The Save-Your-Life Defense Handbook

Books by Matthew Braun

BLACK FOX
MATTIE SILKS
EL PASO
THE SAVAGE LAND
BLOODY HAND
KINCH
CIMARRON JORDAN
NOBLE OUTLAW
BUCK COLTER
THE KINCAIDS

The Save-Your-Life Defense Handbook

by Matt Braun

With sixty action photos

The Devin-Adair Company
Old Greenwich

For information address The Devin-Adair Company,
143 Sound Beach Ave., Old Greenwich, Conn. 06870

Printed in the United States of America

ISBN: 0-8159-5711-4 (hard cover)
0-8159-5712-2 (paperback)

Library of Congress Catalog Card No. 77-71396

Manufactured in the United States of America

Second Printing July, 1980

CONTENTS

To my parents
who taught me the secret
of where to draw the line,
and once having drawn it, never to back off.

INTRODUCTION

The Save-Your-Life Defense Handbook is written for those who need it most, the law-abiding citizens of America. Their need has become so great, in fact, that it is amazing a volume of this nature hasn't appeared before this. Simply stated, Matt Braun's book will equalize the odds between embattled householders and the horde of criminals now rampaging across the nation. It is a straightforward, how-to-do-it manual, written by a man who knows his business—with the single-minded purpose of survival. *Your* survival!

Modern day Americans are a peaceful lot, and understandably so. We have come a long way from the wilderness existence of our forefathers. Yet that frontier life brought about an early familiarity with survival tactics. Pioneer men and women were constantly attacked by Indians, lawless marauders and the vicissitudes of nature. Today, the average American lives in a world of pushbutton conveniences. It is a comfortable life; it is a good life. In most cases, it is a life insulated from the threat of danger or bodily harm.

So it would seem we have lost something in the transition from wilderness hardship to modern technology. On the whole, we are no longer equipped to protect ourselves in a violent situation. Most of us do survive, but only by sheer luck rather than a knowledgeable approach to self-defense and home security. It makes peaceful Americans, therefore, peculiarly vulnerable to attack by the lawless and violent-minded members of our society.

Matt Braun's book pulls no punches. Concise and instructive, it deals with techniques that have withstood the test of life-and-death situations. Citizens and homeowners will discover various methods by which they can successfully defend themselves and save their lives if ever they are assaulted by the modern barbarians who roam our streets.

It would be nice to believe that the information set forth here was not necessary. In a well-ordered, harmonius society, it would not be. However, that is not the type of world we live in. Lenient courts, operating under a philosophy whose shortcomings are catastrophic, have brought about a proliferation of crime, the like of which this nation has never seen. Hardened criminals commit brutal acts of violence, and a year or two later—if not sooner—they are again on the streets. The great majority of them by far continue to murder, assault and rob innocent people, with little fear of either arrest or punishment.

The police, good as they are, cannot be everywhere at once. So the advantage forever falls to the criminal, who strikes while the police are engaged elsewhere. Under those circumstances, unless a man or woman has the information provided by Matt Braun's book, they are virtually helpless against an intruder. However, with this book now available to the public, there is every reason to believe that the odds could change.

A man in the right always has a reservoir of added strength, particularly when he is defending family and home. That knowledge, combined with the techniques supplied by *The Save-Your-Life Defense Handbook,* will at last give the householder an edge over the armed criminal. It is something that this country of ours has long needed.

William Loeb
MANCHESTER, N. H.

1

CRIME AND SELF-DEFENSE

Never send to know for whom
the bell tolls. It tolls for thee.
—John Donne

The Streets of America are No Longer Safe

ON THE heels of the most violent decade in this country's history, blind faith in the brotherhood of man has become a hazardous proposition indeed. The crime rate has risen with frightening swiftness—203% overall—or stated in more chilling terms, an increase each year exceeding 1,000,000 new crimes. One-third of all city dwellers have been victimized in one fashion or another, and even in the suburbs, the figure remains a staggering 20%.

The odds are better than even that at least half of our citizens will be confronted with a potentially violent situation at some point in their lives. Should an individual find himself cast in this unenviable role, he had best know something about self-defense. However sad a commentary, it is nonetheless true that survival has now become a matter of *personal* responsibility. Municipal police and county sheriff departments, which most Americans look to for protection, are charged primarily with law enforcement, *not crime prevention.*

Most states, in fact, legally bar police from entering a situation until a crime has been officially committed. Stated with considerably more personal impact, the police might solve your murder—but rarely, if ever, will they be able to prevent it happening. Los Angeles Chief of Police, Edward Davis, recently underscored the point when he stated that the individual must provide his own and his family's protection. In other words, the police alone can no longer hold down crime.

The fact that some criminals may ultimately be caught provides small consolation for the citizen who has been violated, and none at all for the individual who has been killed. Only 20% of all reported crimes are actually solved, and even then, less than 2% of the felons involved ever see the inside of a prison. A recent poll revealed that a vast majority of Americans view crime on the streets as one of the major problems facing the nation. The survey indicated that 78% of the population feel insecure in their own homes; 80% in large cities are afraid to travel the streets at night; and 70% are willing to pay *more taxes* for increased protection. Columnist Patrick Buchanan went straight to the heart of the problem when he commented, "Those millions of handgun purchases each year represent millions of votes of no confidence by the American people in the criminal justice system of the United States. They are more an effect than a cause of crime. The massive inventory of private weapons is a mountain of testimony to government's utter failure to protect the life, home and property of the average citizen . . . it is the armed criminal, not the armed citizen, whom this country fears."

But how many of the fifty million homeowners who possess guns are knowledgeable of *combat shooting*? Of even greater significance, with one major crime yearly for every twenty-two citizens nationally, can the average homeowner adequately defend himself and his family against an armed criminal? If he doesn't own a gun or is restricted by law from purchasing one (and can't afford $750–$2500 for a trained guard dog), will he know how to use *a knife* or *his hands* with the skills demanded when faced by an assailant?

Newspaper and television reports indicate that the burglar, robber or street thug all too often wins these confrontations. With the incidence of such attacks becoming an ever-increasing aspect of American life, each citizen has ample incentive to more thoroughly inform himself concerning the techniques of self-defense.

Unfortunately, all too many Americans prefer abject submission to resistance. These attitudes are fostered by misguided humanists and self-serving politicians and contribute to a climate in which criminals are free to operate without fear of punishment. So long as we fail individually to make violent crime a hazardous endeavor, the situation will not change.

Violence has now become an all-pervasive aspect in American life, and those who doubt their personal vulnerability need look no further than the daily headlines for proof. Not unlike Biblical writ, what was prophesied has at last come to pass.

Some years ago, the *National Commission on the*

Causes and Prevention of Violence forecast a ghoulish future for urban areas across the nation. Contained in the report was an ominous prediction: unless the rampant crime rate was checked, downtown areas would soon become deserted after dark except for police patrols; apartment buildings and business establishments would require the protection of armed private guards; entire cities populated by terrified citizens would become possessed of a fortress mentality. The paranoia of such a future is no longer conjecture. It is today's reality.

Large business firms, such as banks and department stores, are currently building inside parking garages to protect employees from mugging and rape. Churches are hiring guards to ride "shotgun" for ushers who have been repeatedly robbed after taking the Sunday collection. Restaurants and theaters in major cities are closing early because the public refuses to walk the downtown area after dark. Private security agencies now enjoy such a rush of business that many are forced to turn away customers, and a rash of kennels have surfaced across the country in response to the public's demand for attack-trained watchdogs.

In metropolitan areas (and increasingly in the suburbs) people literally "fort up" for the night behind locked doors and barred windows. It is an old and honorable custom: medieval barons dug moats, and our forefathers built stockades to protect themselves from marauders who roamed the countryside. But while we have regressed to the fortress concept, we have eliminated its most vital element. In most cities the householder is restricted—under penalty of imprisonment—in the use of weapons to defend himself and his property.

Yet fear is clearly afoot in America, and all indications point to the situation becoming progressively worse within the next decade. Whether or not federal, state and local authorities can devise adequate methods to protect the life and property of *all* citizens remains a moot question; the problem continues to confound even the experts. In the meantime, the individual is still faced with the prospect of a hoodlum attacking him on the streets or invading his home. For the person who is incapable of providing his own self-defense, those prospects appear disturbing indeed.

The problem is compounded by the fact that our overburdened judicial system has now taken on all the aspects of a house built on sand. Inexorably, the courts are sinking into a morass of criminal cases so vast that apathy rather than action has become the most noticeable characteristic. Criminals are immune to justice simply by manipulating the expediences of our system: low bail and slick lawyers; harried prosecutors who are anxious to plea bargain; and judges so overworked they are willing to grant probation just to get the case off the books. The thought assumes even more unsettling undertones when one notes that of all *major* crimes reported only 12% lead to arrest, barely 6% result in a conviction, and less than 2% of convicted felons are actually sent to prison.

With appalling frequency, repeat offenders are being turned back on the street due to a stark fact: our jails are inadequate to hold the legion of men charged with committing violent crimes each day. The odds of serving time for a serious crime— *including murder*—are approximately three in a hundred! Thus, for citizens who have been robbed, raped or assaulted, the process of bringing their assailant to justice quickly becomes a study in frustration and disillusionment. In large cities it is commonplace for a victim to wait a year or longer before his assailant can be brought to trial. The ordeal is interminable, not to say grueling, and a great many of those victimized simply drop the charges in disgust. Understandably, the public now harbors serious doubt as to the power of the courts to punish, much less deter, criminals.

In sprawling, crime infested Los Angeles, a store owner who has killed one hoodlum and wounded another in the course of being robbed sixteen times was recently asked which method he considered the most effective in combating holdups: burglar alarms, guard dogs (he has two German shepherds) or guns? His response revealed the rather frightening plight, wherever one lives, of an entire nation: "You need them all."

Even the politicians and liberal do-gooders are now admitting, in print, that the "dream of rehabilitation has failed." The "cures" tried haven't worked, and because of crowded courts and overflowing prisons, the most dangerous criminals are often allowed to go free. "The plain fact is that we do not know what to do about violent crime, so we often end up talking big and doing nothing."

How true! But it really comes as no great surprise to the average citizen. Current public mood toward the death penalty provides an excellent barometer regarding the failure of our judicial system. Ten years ago the majority of Americans were against imposing the "extreme" sentence. Today, with horror stories of terrorism and mass murder flooding the headlines, 71% of the public favors reinstatement of the death penalty. Quite obviously, America has had enough of the "enlightened experiment" in rehabilitation; that spirit is reflected in recent decisions handed down by the Supreme Court. Unfortunately, it took a decade of senseless violence to convince the idealists that a slap on the wrist merely invites further aggression.

So now, having failed miserably in their grand experiment, the bleedinghearts would have us believe that gun control is the cure-all for what ails our society. At the forefront of this antigun faction are several ambitious politicians—of the lean and hungry type—who once again hope to beguile the public with emotional appeals and specious logic. If devious, they are at least explicit about their ultimate goal: the confiscation of *all* guns in the United States. That goal is a matter of public record, and when devious men (especially politicians) speak with such candor, the American people would be wise to take them at their word.

Yet these same politicians, who virtually demolished our judicial system, have once more chosen to ignore reality. Like a sleight-of-hand artist, they hope to focus your attention on the symptom rather than the cause. If you find that statement perhaps too partisan, then merely ask yourself a few obvious questions.

Will confiscating the guns of law-abiding citizens affect the crime rate? *NOTE:* Less than 1/100 of 1% of legal gun owners are involved in felonious crime.

Who is it that actually uses guns in the commission of crime? *NOTE:* Nearly 80% of all gun-related crimes are committed by previously convicted felons.

Will those same criminals obligingly surrender their guns if restrictive legislation is enacted? *NOTE:* In New York City alone, where stringent gun control has been in effect since 1911, there are an estimated 1,000,000 unregistered handguns. Anyone with the right price can purchase a *hot* pistol, totally untraceable, within a matter of hours.

If laws are enacted denying you a gun, will the police be able to protect you from armed criminals? *NOTE:* In several cities where rape and robbery were epidemic, the crime rate plummeted after local police trained women and store owners in the use of firearms. Had it been illegal for honest citizens to own guns, the crime rate would have obviously soared ever higher.

Will Americans docilely surrender their guns to Big Brother? *NOTE:* The consensus of several public polls is that Americans would consider this an abridgment of their Constitutional rights. Experts estimate it would require not just a police state, but a door-to-door campaign by the military, to enforce gun confiscation.

Are you willing to live in a society where *only* the police and the military are allowed to possess firearms? *NOTE:* Tyrants never allow their subjects to own weapons; the first step is to disarm the citizenry. Free men remain free only so long as they are capable of defending themselves; Soviet Russia and Nazi Germany provide classic illustrations of the abuse of power.

Finally, we must ask ourselves the most fundamental of all questions. Have we forgotten the bitter lesson of our *first and last* experiment in prohibition? If Congress bans the ownership of guns in America, then foreign manufacturers would be delighted to glut the market with cheap, smuggled imports. Organized Crime got its start bootlegging whiskey, and by bootlegging guns it would merely become richer—and stronger. In a very real and chilling sense, a vote for gun control is a vote for the Mafia.

Of still greater consequence, it is the American taxpayer who would suffer the financial burden necessary for the proper enforcement of restrictive gun laws. Yet another bureaucratic monolith would be created to register, license and/or confiscate guns—and the price tag would be staggering. In New York City, the cost to investigate and process one application for a pistol license exceeds $100. On a national scale, the cost to taxpayers is estimated at upwards of $5 billion. The Federal government could literally dictate to the populace, and the bureaucrats would have again feathered their own nest. Meanwhile, the honest citizen (ultimately stripped of pistol, rifle and shotgun) would be left to face an armed criminal and shout that timeless plea of desperation: "Where the hell are the police when you need them?"

All of which merits one last thought on New York's fabled Sullivan Law. It was *never* a law designed to protect the public, or reduce crime, nor was it enacted at the request of the police. It was politically motivated, engineered to protect the party machine of New York City. In 1911, the late Tim Sullivan bulldozed his restrictive act—banning possession and/or ownership of a handgun without a police permit—through the state legislature. The elections that followed came off precisely as planned. Sullivan's henchmen were armed and the opposition's poll watchers found themselves at a distinct disadvantage. Who's to say that we don't have several modern counterparts of Tim Sullivan in Washington today? Perhaps the gun control legislation before Congress is designed not to protect the public, or reduce crime, but rather to protect the bureaucracy and those who covet still greater power. Though it's a shopworn cliché, it is nonetheless true that history does have a way of repeating itself.

Think about it a moment. The Sullivan Law is another classic example of how bureaucrats can pervert the legislative process to their own ends. Now ask yourself one final question. Would you entrust the future of your country and your personal freedom to the whims of some political hack in the years ahead?

If so, then slide over. Big Brother is about to move in.

On the other hand, maybe you're a realist instead of an idealist. Perhaps you can recognize the truth when you hear it, and prefer to follow the credo of Los Angeles Police Chief Edward Davis, who recently stated, "I am going to keep my home armed and anybody who wants my guns will have to come and get them the hard way! What other protection do I have? There's not a police department big enough and well-staffed enough to guarantee citizens it can safeguard them. . . ."

Aside from the pros and cons of gun ownership, there is a consideration of graver magnitude concerning the entire spectrum of self-defense. Under common law, which prevails in most states, there is a catchall phrase called *deadly force.* Stripped of legalese, deadly force simply means the manner—gun, knife, club or bare hands—that you use to kill an assailant. Common law states that a person assailed in his own home does not have to retreat. If the intruder presents a reasonable threat of death or bodily harm, then deadly force is legally permissible. But take care, and beware, of that word *reasonable.* Prosecutors and judges in every state give it varying connotations, and under the wrong circumstances, it could buy you a term in prison.

Common law decrees that deadly force cannot be used solely to protect property. In other words, it would be highly ill-advised to shoot an *unarmed* burglar, even though he's on his way out the window with the family jewels and your color TV. If he had a gun or a knife and made a threatening move, that's another matter altogether. Common law does permit the use of deadly force against a violent intruder. Yet that force cannot be used unless there is *reasonable* fear by the homeowner for his personal safety or the safety of his family.

What constitutes *reasonable* fear? How do you prove violent intent without allowing an intruder the edge—that first threatening move? How do you protect yourself against bodily harm without waiting to be assaulted or killed? There has never been a definitive answer, by any court in this nation, to those questions. Yet it is said that dead men tell no tales, and in every police station in the country, there are stories of a deceased burglar found with the family carving knife in his hand. So if you blow away the friendly neighborhood burglar, you had better make damned sure he was armed, and it wouldn't hurt to have a couple of reliable witnesses to support your version of the encounter. Otherwise you might find yourself explaining the affair in great detail to a judge and jury.

Perhaps that sounds inequitable. Almost as though the

burglar/robber/rapist has a greater right to life, liberty and the pursuit of happiness than you or your family. Under today's judicial system, which might be termed "bassackward," there is no doubt whatever that you defend yourself at your own peril. Contrary to the historical premise of common law, if you kill an assailant on the street or in your home, you are often *presumed guilty* until you prove yourself innocent. As a case in point, I once spent a heated afternoon with a district attorney and his staff (the city will remain nameless) concerning the legality of carrying a sheathed Commando fighting knife. Only after three hours and several harsh exchanges would the district attorney admit that it was not against the law to carry the knife. It became illegal only if the knife was used in the commission of a felony. Which does not include *reasonable deadly force* in a situation of self-defense.

In retrospect, I have often wondered how many honest people lost their lives in that city simply because they thought it illegal to walk the streets armed with anything larger than a four-inch pocket knife. I also wonder whether the district attorney in question is able to sleep at night. By propagating false information, he does nothing to deter muggers or rapists, but he does inhibit law-abiding citizens from employing a means of self-defense that is both justifiable and legal. So it seems that the law is, after all, sometimes inequitable. Or perhaps it's all in the eye of the beholder. Particularly if the beholder *supports* your story in every detail.

But take heart! Oliver Wendell Holmes wrote in a 1921 Supreme Court decision: "Detached reflection cannot be demanded in the presence of an uplifted knife." In a tight situation, that sage opinion would doubtless sway even the sternest of judges.

Another pearl of wisdom, attributed to a deputy sheriff, was equally succinct: "Better to be judged by twelve than carried by six." Anyone who needs an interpretation of the statement would be well-advised to consider passive submission rather than self-defense.

Then there's the California man whose actions declare loud and strong that the American spirit is still alive and well. In a concise, forceful letter, he wrote: "I was the victim in an attempted robbery-murder, and am very lucky to be alive now (I was stabbed twice in the chest and had my head split open). The reason I am alive now is because I had a handgun . . . and the knowledge of how to use it. One of my assailants is now dead, the other has been found guilty of murder in the first degree, attempted murder and attempted armed robbery. But for the fact that I was armed, I too would be dead. . . ."

Never has it been better stated. It is, in fact, the very marrow of this book—a book directed to the millions of men and women who have grown disgusted with cringing in fear, and have resolved at last to do something about their own protection.

The HANDBOOK is devoted to the three primary means of self-defense most commonly available to the homeowner or man on the street: gunfighting, knife fighting, and hand-to-hand combat. The techniques illustrated are quick, brutal and extremely practical. Though these methods might initially seem callous, they provide the only realistic approach to adequate self-defense.

Peaceful citizens would do well to bear in mind that the street thug is already well versed in the use of guns, knives and dirty fighting. The criminal will find nothing especially new in the pages to follow. But law-abiding men and women will discover methods which can provide them with a fighting chance should the need arise to protect themselves.

However much a man may abhor the thought, it is a fact of modern-day life that our streets, as well as our homes, are no longer safe. Anyone attacked by a wild animal wouldn't hesitate to use whatever means are necessary to defend himself; a mugger, robber or rapist is no less bestial, and all too often considerably more savage than a wild animal. Harsh as it sounds, today's breed of street thug deserves whatever he gets; it is his total disregard for human life that makes him the most dangerous creature ever to stalk the weak and the unwary. And faced with survival in an age of pervasive violence, the distasteful yet deadly skills discussed in this HANDBOOK represent the best odds an individual is likely to obtain.

That very point was recently demonstrated in an experiment conducted in Highland Park, a suburban community outside of Detroit. Confronted with nearly 550 armed robberies over the past year, city police launched a program of handgun instruction for local merchants. The goal was to train businessmen to protect themselves and their businesses from robbers, and the program was given wide publicity throughout the metropolitan area. In four months the store-robbery rate plummeted from an average of 1.5 a day to *none.* All of which rather graphically illustrates the premise of this HANDBOOK.

A people trained to defend themselves—and willing to meet a criminal on his own terms—need have no fear of violent encounters. Like all predators, a hoodlum seldom hunts anything that will fight back.

And the choice is yours.

2

HOME SECURITY

Set thine house in order.
—Isaiah, 38:1

Home Sweet Home Has Become an Endangered Species

OVER THE past decade residential burglaries have increased 286%. Yesterday there was a burglary every 13 seconds. A woman was raped every 2 minutes. Someone was murdered every 28 minutes. Tomorrow it gets worse!

So it appears that your home is no longer your castle. Nor is it a sanctuary or a refuge or even a place of safety. Any door, any window, any lock can be breached. All of which means that your life and property are only slightly more secure at home than on the street.

To ensure absolute security against intruders would require nothing less than a fort. To profess otherwise is to ignore the hundreds of thousands of crimes committed every year. So don't kid yourself. Your home is vulnerable at all times! Whether you're on the premises or out for the evening hardly matters. Burglars regularly cruise your neighborhood, and if they haven't yet hit your house, don't rejoice. It's merely a matter of time.

The experienced burglar—let's call him the Old Pro—is a master craftsman. He can open a locked door and slip inside almost as fast as the homeowner does with a key. Of course, since the public is so accommodating, he normally doesn't have to bother. People carefully lock all doors and windows, and then forget an outside basement entrance or a connecting door to the garage. The oversight greatly simplifies things for the Old Pro, but in the long run it's probably of little consequence. He would have gotten inside anyhow, regardless of your precautions, and done it without leaving a trace.

On the other hand, the average household has nothing to fear from the Old Pro. Always the professional, he's a man of discrimination and keen judgment. Wealthy homes and businesses are his lodestone; seldom does he waste his expertise on trifles. It takes a haul worth thousands—jewelry and furs, cash and valuable merchandise—before he'll risk a job. So most of us are safe from the Old Pro. In a sense, we're beneath him. Simply not worth the effort.

All of which places us in a category of "higher risk."

The Old Pro is a phantom, ultracool and wary of any contact with his "clients." Rather than chance violent confrontation, he'll head for the nearest exit and quickly vanish. But the everyday "working" burglar is an altogether different matter. He's an opportunist and a hustler, and he generally knocks over several homes in any given week. A dark house with no car in the driveway—any house that appears unoccupied—will immediately attract his attention. Like a lowly chicken thief, his ambitions are modest. He's after the quick score—stereos, television sets, guns—easily disposable items that will turn a fast buck. Never to be confused with the Old Pro, he's a ripoff specialist, strictly hit-and-run.

And he's a hazard to your health.

Lacking finesse, he will jimmy a door or break a window to gain entrance. Seldom does he have a plan; more often than not, he goes in cold, without any knowledge of the house or its occupants. His methods are sloppy, he relies heavily on luck, and in all probability, he's armed. If detected, he might run. Or then again, he might not. To avoid being caught, he often kills, and it's not at all uncommon for a wife to be raped while her husband lies dead in the hallway.

Incredibly, still another factor contributes to the likelihood of violence. With increasing frequency, today's burglar is also a drug addict. Since an addict must steal to support his habit—upwards of $100 a day at street prices—that means he must burgle one or more homes every day. Thus, a single addict will commit several hundred burglaries a year, and there are literally thousands of addicts looking to "score" at any given moment. Which accounts for the skyrocketing crime rate in the suburbs and small towns. The man with a monkey on his back has become a commuter; he now roams the countryside in the dual role of burglar and/or armed robber. And a junkie in need of a fix is a very unstable character. He needs that loot—*needs it desperately*—and if you get in his way, he won't hesitate. ***He'll kill you.***

Then there are the crazies. Not true thieves, yet infinitely more dangerous. Generally, he's a psycho who becomes a burglar/rapist/killer out of compulsion rather than by design. Perhaps he poses as a salesman or a repairman—the Boston Strangler used several disguises—and gains entrance merely by ringing the doorbell. Or perhaps he simply invades your home, armed with a knife or gun, and proceeds to act out the nightmare. The Sharon Tate murders were a bizarre example, but hardly an isolated incident. It happens with chilling frequency across America. So often, in fact, that we're no longer startled by reports of the latest slaughter. Instead, we've come to expect it, shrug it off. Merely one of the random horrors that happen to other people but *never* to us.

In truth, it can happen to anyone. Random violence is like a bolt of lightning. It strikes without reason or personal animosity. Yet the victims are no less dead, and oddly enough, those who believe it could never happen are usually the very ones killed.

A brief aside. Early last spring a car with out-of-state plates pulled into the driveway. There were four men in the car, and they sat staring at the house, talking among themselves. Since I live in the mountains—on a road that literally goes nowhere—it's difficult to get there by accident. Several summer homes had already been burglarized that spring; police had caught some burglars, and *all* were from a major city across the state line. My own car was in the garage, so the house appeared unoccupied. To the four men, it apparently had the look of a perfect set-up. All of them crawled out of the car and walked toward the house.

I stuck a pistol in my waistband and snapped a short leash on my Malamute. The dog weighs slightly over 100 lbs. and has a very nasty disposition toward strangers. We stepped outside and greeted our unexpected guests. They came to a halt—four grungy-looking types in their early twenties—eyes glued on the dog (now growling) and the gun. To my inquiry, one of them replied that they were looking for the "Wilson" family. I informed them

The Malamute. A one-family watchdog with a very nasty disposition. Suspicious of all strangers and a hazard to the health of any intruder.

that there were no Wilsons within twenty miles, and then added, "Boys, you picked the wrong house." Apparently they couldn't have agreed more. All smiles, they hurriedly jumped in the car and departed.

Of course, some people would say I overreacted and scared the hell out of four innocent youths. Others would conclude that it was a display of machismo on my part. Unfortunately, these are the very people who get struck by lightning—and random violence.

The point is quite simple. Somebody else got burglarized that day. I didn't. After a call to the state police, the four men were apprehended late that afternoon. Their car was loaded with loot, and they were headed back to the big city. So draw your own conclusions. Then take a moment to reflect on man's obligation to protect himself and his family and his home.

It could very well happen to you.

In fact, given the crime rate, it probably will. None of us is immune, and our homes are always vulnerable. Worse, today's burglar often resorts to senseless violence. Not just psychos and drug addicts either. All too frequently the semi-pro burglar kills merely to eliminate witnesses. Thus, you can never assume that an intruder means you no harm. Instead, you would be wise to assume just the opposite and prepare yourself for that eventuality. Vigilance is no longer an antiquated concept. It's very much the "in" thing these days, and late some night, when you're awakened by a strange noise, it could save your life.

On that note, with vigilance uppermost in mind, we come to the basic premise of home security. *There is no way you can prevent an intruder from gaining entrance to your house.* Yet there are several ways to slow him down or frighten him off or trap him. And finally, there's the last resort. A contingency plan, designed especially for the armed intruder who relies on violence to complete the job. Before committing yourself to the last resort, however, there are various alternative measures you may wish to consider. None is foolproof, and some have definite limitations, but all of them merit careful thought.

LOCKS

One of the great misconceptions of our time is the "burglar-proof" lock. We tend to forget that *most* burglars are bright, innovative people, highly flexible in a cunning sort of way. Anything a lock manufacturer can design, the burglar will ultimately devise a method to circumvent. Of course, some locks are extremely complicated and will stymie the ripoff artist. But if he's determined, then he simply goes to work on the door itself or else switches to a window. One way or another, he can gain entry. To illustrate the point, perhaps a brief review of the burglar's methods are in order.

The average household has a common tumbler lock with a spring-loaded bolt. With the door closed, the bolt seats into a recess in the door frame. Once the bolt is disengaged—and on this lock there's only *one* bolt—the door swings open at the touch of a finger. These locks can be "carded" (by pressing a stiff credit card between the bolt and the door frame) or "slipped" in a similar manner with a pen knife or screwdriver. Start to finish, the whole operation requires about ten seconds. Maybe double that if it's a clumsy burglar.

Some homeowners have gone to the dead bolt design, since the bolt is seated mechanically and cannot be carded or slipped. Others rely on the mortise lock; or key-in-the-knob locks with trigger bolts; or the vertical-bolt auxiliary lock. Yet all of these locks offer only a moderate challenge to the skilled burglar. With a set of lock picks and a bit of experience, it's relatively easy to outwit even the most advanced design.

Aside from carding and picks, there's always jimmying, the burglar's old standby. Jimmying consists of wedging a prybar or a heavy-duty screwdriver between the door and the jamb, and forcing them apart. Or if noise is a factor, then he simply performs a little surgery on the nearest window with a suction cup and a glass cutter. In the suburbs, window surgery has been perfected to a near science.

Not to belittle the ingenuity of manufacturers, there is a variety of alarm locks and push-button sequence locks and keyless binary-coded locks. But as a practical matter, most homeowners will consider the cost prohibitive, and thus it becomes a moot issue.

So we return at last to the old stockade concept. If you're home, put a stout safety chain on the door and then batten it down with a horizontal cross bar. (Burglary has become so epidemic that several companies now market both a horizontal bar-lock and a floor-to-door bar-lock.) Short of a sledgehammer or a battering ram, the burglar will have met his match. Even then, unless you live in an apartment building, he still has the option of windows or a patio door. Which leads us, by virtue of the burglar's determination, to your second line of defense.

ALARM SYSTEMS

A decade ago anyone who had a burglar alarm in his home was considered a bit eccentric. Or else so wealthy that he was a prime candidate on the Old Pro's hit list. Without a mass market, there was no incentive for manufacturers to upgrade technology and convert to volume production. Thus alarm systems were complex, difficult to install, and enormously expensive.

Our explosive crime rate changed all that, of course, and slowly gave birth to a whole new industry. On the market today are any number of moderately priced alarm systems. A homeowner can install the unit himself, simply by following instructions, and little if any maintenance is required. Nor is he any longer thought to be an eccentric. The experience of a friend, who lives outside Boston, typifies the plight of all homeowners. After his house was ransacked seven times in less than a year, he ordered installation of the most advanced system available. It put a large dent on his bankroll, but he hasn't been burglarized since.

Naturally, the more complex the system, the higher the cost. Yet it's become an extremely competitive industry, and nearly any homeowner can find a unit to fit his budget. Basically, there are four types of alarm systems suitable for home use; some require professional installation, others do not. Your best bet is to consult the Yellow Pages and call a firm specializing in home security. However, a brief review will give you some idea of cost and the wide selection available.

Conductive Tape. An electrical circuit flows through a network of conductive tape which covers all points of entry. Normally, this system is mounted on windows; any attempt to break the glass will interrupt the current and trigger an alarm. Complete security requires that additional contacts be mounted along the edge of windows and doors. If desired, the system can be tied into the local police station, and automatically alerts officers of a break-in. It's elaborate but costly—generally in excess of $1000—and the average homeowner may find the price tag prohibitive.

Electric Eye. In this system, photoelectric sensors detect the entrance of an intruder. A constant light source is beamed to a photoelectric cell; if the beam is interrupted, then the sensor activates an alarm. Although excellent for guarding doors and hallways, complete home security with this system requires dozens of sensors as well as professional installation. Unless the sensors are strategically placed and well concealed, the savvy burglar would find it relatively easy to bypass the entire system. So cost becomes a big factor—very big—perhaps out of reach for the average homeowner.

Ultrasonic Sound. A highly sophisticated system which projects inaudible sound waves in a cone-shaped pattern. So long as there is no *movement* within the field of sound, nothing happens. Once the field is interrupted, however, reflected sound waves bounce back to the unit and trigger an alarm. The device itself is small and portable—usually disguised as a book or stereo speaker—and as a result, very inconspicuous. All of the units currently available can be adjusted for sensitivity; to the point, in fact, that a mosquito or a house fly will activate the alarm.

Some models are also available with a battery power pack, but most simply plug into a wall socket. The unit can be rigged to activate either a lamp or radio while it simultaneously triggers an external siren. It's extremely versatile and moderately priced; one unit, strategically placed, will outwit any burglar. Wherever he gains entry—through a door or through a window—his mere *presence* in a room will activate the entire system.

Circuit Breakers. An inexpensive system designed to cover all points of entry. Small magnetic contacts, wired to a battery-operated alarm, are attached to window/window frame and door/door frame throughout the house. When a window is raised or a door opened, the circuit is broken and instantly triggers the alarm. The control box can be rigged for "at home" or "away from home" operation; the unit also has a manually operated "panic" button for use at bedside. If basic, it's nonetheless very reliable, and can be installed by the homeowner in a couple of hours. Moreover, the unit is quite economical—$100 or less—which places it within the budget of nearly everyone.

The city dweller or suburbanite will find one of these four basic systems adequate to his needs. The rural homeowner, however, has an altogether different problem. With the advent of the commuter burglar, and vandals even mounted on snowmobiles, a country home no longer enjoys immunity. If anything, the isolation works to the burglar's advantage. It allows him to take his time, and virtually eliminates the risk of his being observed.

To be effective, security systems for rural homes require elaborate planning. Since neighbors and the police are usually too far away to help, the homeowner must rely on himself and his own ingenuity. Intruder alarms should be located in both the main house and outbuildings; if possible, the system should activate one or more sirens as well as outside floodlights. As an alternative, wire a single switch inside the house that will flood the entire property with light. The combination of screeching sirens and blinding floodlights will usually convince a burglar to take off and not look back.

Yet there are no guarantees. So never *assume* he'll run.

Since I live in a remote section of mountains, my own security system operates by stages. Once activated, the sequence steadily escalates the danger to a burglar. An ultrasonic proximity alarm triggers several ear-splitting wailer horns. One inside light switch instantly transforms midnight to sunrise all around the property. An intruder already inside the house encounters still another obstacle, in the form of a very large and very hostile Malamute. If he succeeds in getting past the dog—or getting away from the dog—then he faces the ultimate hurdle: a double-barrel shotgun I keep loaded at bedside.

All of which says a good deal about burglar alarms. However sophisticated, an alarm system merely alerts you to the presence of an intruder. Perhaps it will frighten him off. Then again, perhaps it won't. And of course, there's always the chance of a malfunction. Discounting nothing, we come then to that most ancient early warning device: Man's Best Friend.

THE WATCHDOG

Dogs can be trained to bark or guard or attack. The key word, however, is *trained.* So never confuse one trait with another when considering a dog for the security of your household. A *good* watchdog is an excellent deterrent to burglars. But good watchdogs aren't born—they're trained!

Contrary to legend, not all dogs are fierce defenders of

home and hearth. Nor will the family pet always come to the aid of the family. Like people, dogs possess very definite character traits. Some are brave and resourceful, absolutely fearless when danger threatens. Others prefer flight to fight, and invariably watch the action from a safe distance. Even in the canine world, there are lovers and there are fighters. And sometimes, if you're lucky, your dog has it all.

Several years ago, a woman in Alaska was attacked by a Kodiak bear. Her St. Bernard not only came to the rescue, but drove the bear off and sent it high-tailing for the woods. A few months later, in Los Angeles, a woman was raped and murdered by a housebreaker. The police found her Great Dane cowering underneath the kitchen table. Which is not to say that your dog would slink off and hide. Perhaps he would attack man or bear in your defense. But unless Rover has been trained for the job, don't stake your life on it.

In fact, before you buy a dog for home security, there are several factors to consider. If all you want is a barker—an animate alarm system—then probably any dog will do. But if you want a genuine watchdog—one who defends person and property—then you have to ask yourself some very serious questions, not the least of which has to do with time and expense and how much responsibility you're willing to accept. Essentially, it comes down to a choice between a barker and a biter, and it's not a decision to be made lightly.

The House Dog. All you can safely assume about the house dog is that he will warn you of intruders. Any dog, regardless of breed, has the "territorial" instinct. While he might run under the bed, he will usually bark if a strange presence enters the house at night. Most dogs, even when left alone in the house, will bark if an intruder attempts to enter. But not *all* dogs! The waggly-tail variety will whine and kiss a burglar's hand while he loots your house. Still, almost any statement is a generalization. Unless you've *trained* the dog to bark, it could go either way.

On the other hand, it's possible to train almost any large, aggressive dog and convert him into a true watchdog. The Malamute mentioned earlier was purchased at age seven weeks. From the outset, I wrestled and fought with him, and encouraged his natural aggressive tendencies. At age four months I began his obedience training. (Nearly all cities have one or more obedience schools and there are several excellent books on obedience training.) By voice command and demonstration, I constantly encouraged the dog to become suspicious of *all* strangers. Then, with the help of a gutsy friend, I taught him to attack *if* I was assaulted. Today, the dog distrusts *everyone* outside my immediate family. He responds instantly to voice control, but otherwise he is vicious and challenges anyone who comes to the door.

Keep in mind, this is a *one-family* watchdog. I purposely encouraged him to become ferocious, and thus, I alone bear the responsibility for his actions. If friends come to visit, the dog gets locked in the cellar. Unless he's with me, the dog is never allowed outside; he would threaten anyone who comes on the property. Also, if I had children, I would *never* train a dog in this manner, and I suggest you reflect on that statement at length. Still, as a watchdog, the Malamute suits my needs perfectly. An intruder, once inside the house, would have to kill the dog in order to escape. And if either my wife or I were attacked, the assailant would find himself in a fight for his life.

The way I've trained my dog is one man's choice. It works for me, but I would recommend it to very few people. A "home trained" watchdog is *not* trustworthy around strangers, children or friends. Unless you have rapport with dogs, and the will to command obedience, then discard the idea entirely. For the homeowner with small children, it really narrows down to training a feisty "barker" who will sound the alarm on intruders. Of course, if you're determined to have a watchdog, there are a couple of alternatives. Both are quite expensive, and by no means suitable for every household, but it's your option.

The Area Guard Dog. Usually a Doberman or German shepherd, the area guard dog is a specialist. Not unlike a sentry, he has been trained to patrol and guard a *particular area.* In most instances the area is a factory or business establishment; on occasion, an estate or fenced property would be suitable. However, a guard dog for private use poses grave problems.

Bear in mind that an area guard dog operates independently. Once a handler places him on guard, the dog roams free and functions without further commands. Any person the dog *has not* been trained to accept looms as a menace to his assigned area and triggers an automatic response. In a sense, the dog has been programmed by professional trainers to *attack and neutralize* any intruder. Further, if an intruder struggles or attempts to escape, the dog will literally rip him apart. So the dog reacts instantly—without command—whenever an intruder enters his assigned area. And the dog considers *everyone* except his handler, or owner, to be an intruder.

Thus it becomes apparent that an area guard dog must be *contained.* Either a fence or high wall is essential; allowed to run loose, the dog would threaten and/or attack anyone who happens along. In short, the area guard dog is dangerous to *all* outsiders. Think of him as a miniature Bengal tiger. He's aggressive and vicious—absolutely fearless—and capable of savage ferocity. There are simply no mitigating circumstances once the dog challenges a stranger. He's been trained to do one thing, and he does it exceedingly well.

Jerrold Mundis, author of *The Guard Dog,* and one of America's leading authorities on the subject, states categorically that an area guard dog should never be considered by the average homeowner. The risk to family, friends and neighbors is simply too great; one mishap could result in a severe mauling, possibly death, and of course, the inevitable law suit. According to Mundis, an area guard dog becomes practical only on an estate or large private property. Even then, the grounds must be enclosed by a security fence or high wall, and the dog must be taught to accept the family as part of his assignment. Otherwise the dog would consider them no different from a common intruder.

All things considered, an area guard dog in the home could become a liability—or worse! Aside from the cost of the dog—generally $750 or more—there's the danger factor. An area dog receives minimal obedience training; his feral instincts are purposely honed to a sort of hair-trigger paranoia, and it's no easy task to control such an animal. He's one tough cookie—and he knows it! It's all business and no play, and he merely lives for the day that someone tries to climb *his* fence. On the other hand, if you own a lavish estate, then an area guard dog is far superior to any burglar alarm ever invented. Assuming you recognize the problems involved, and never shirk the responsibility, your home will be well protected indeed. And for a really peaceful night's sleep, you may want to consider the area dog's ugly brother.

The Command Attack Dog. By definition, the attack dog is a dangerous and highly lethal weapon. On command, he will attack anything—man or beast—regardless of the odds. There are documented instances of attack dogs, mortally wounded by gunshot, who still neutralized the assailant. So in a very real sense, ordering an attack dog into action is little different from squeezing the trigger on a pistol. The attack, by law, would be consid-

The Command Attack Dog. Lots of teeth and a voracious attitude toward intruders. Always on duty, very reliable, and far superior to any burglar alarm. (*Photo by Jerrold Mundis.*)

ered use of deadly force, and the dog's owner would bear full responsibility.

Of course, there is an essential difference between attack dogs and other weapons. A bullet cannot be stopped or recalled once fired; an attack dog can be called off and put on guard once he has immobilized an assailant. The key factor is one of command. An attack dog *will not* attack of his own volition. A large part of his training is devoted to discipline and self-control; even when provoked, the dog will not attack without orders. In that sense, he is actually safer and more trustworthy than a common house dog. Yet once he's *commanded* to attack, the dog becomes a brute destructive force—utterly merciless, and capable of inflicting mortal wounds.

Naturally, under extraordinary circumstances, the control factor no longer applies. If the dog's master is assaulted, and has no chance to order attack, the dog will attack, without an instant's hesitation. In the event the dog's master is surprised and knocked unconscious, and therefore unable to call the dog off, the situation could become very messy indeed. An attack dog's jaws exert 750 lbs. of pressure (sufficient to sever a finger or crush an armbone) and his fangs literally can tear a man to shreds. Without exaggeration, it is the equivalent of feeding an assailant into a large, very efficient meatgrinder.

Clearly, the decision to buy an attack dog is one of some consequence. Aside from the question of deadly force, there's the initial cost to be considered. Any reputable trainer will charge $1000–$2500 for an attack dog, which represents a major investment for the average homeowner. Amortized over a period of years, the investment becomes quite reasonable, approximately $20 per month. However, it's still a hefty chunk of cash to lay out in a lump sum.

Then there's the matter of time. Overall you should figure on one to three months to complete the training. A Doberman or German shepherd is an intelligent animal, but the time factor depends to a great extent on your own competence with dogs. The trainer will insist that you participate in both the obedience training and the attack training. In this manner, the dog's allegiance and trust are transferred to you, and only then do *you* become his master. Nor does the time factor end with the dog's formal training. You must continue to reinforce his "education" with periodic training sessions of your own. *NOTE:* Beware of buying a "secondhand" attack dog. The program of retraining necessary to make him *your* dog is both time-consuming and costly—and you might never win his complete loyalty.

An attack dog invariably makes an affectionate family pet. Since he has been taught to attack *only* on command, he's unusually safe around children and friends. However, you must introduce him into the family, and condition him to accept them as part of his assignment. Moreover, if you're away from home a good deal, then your wife should participate in his formal training. Afterwards, even in your absence, she will be able to command "attack" with a high degree of authority.

Thus, as a practical matter, the attack dog's value is dependent upon the presence of his master. Or mistress. Control is vital, and without it, the dog has wide latitude in how he reacts to any given situation. So consider carefully, and weigh the alternatives, before you buy yourself a resident juggernaut. It's no small responsibility.

By now, you've probably gathered that Man's Best Friend has certain limitations with regard to home security. Perhaps the greatest limitation is his master. Whether you choose a feisty barker, a guard dog or an attack dog, his effectiveness is the product of your patience and your rapport with animals. Don't expect the dog to do it all on his own, strictly from instinct, and don't expect the professional trainer to create an infallible guardian of home and hearth. A watchdog is only as reliable as his master, and in large measure, he's a reflection of your own character. Long ago, a homespun philosopher summed it up with one pithy remark:

"Watch a man's dog, and you'll soon know the man."

A WORD TO SENIOR CITIZENS

The plight of the nation's Senior Citizens is particularly grim. Often trapped in the inner cities, either by economic circumstance or reluctance to leave the old neighborhood, they have become prime targets for burglars and roving street gangs. Nationwide, nine out of every 1000 elderly have been victimized. Yet, appalling as it is, the statistical story is merely the tip of the iceberg. The problem has become so acute that the aged now live in a state of semi-siege—barricaded in their homes—terrified to travel the streets even in broad daylight.

In street jargon, crimes against Senior Citizens are jokingly called "crib jobs." Hoodlums feel it's like taking candy from a baby; the elderly are often weak and vulnerable, frequently incapable of resistance. Worse, police officials confirm that criminals who prey on the aged have become increasingly vicious—even sadistic—in their attacks. It is not at all unusual for women in their 70s to be raped. Beatings are now commonplace, and the specter of murder is ever present. One youthful offender, age 20, was recently charged with beating and robbing an 82-year-old woman. Investigation revealed that he had a voluminous record—sixty-seven prior arrests—including one for the murder of a 92-year-old man. He was released on bail, which says a great deal about our criminal justice system.

Perhaps the plight of all Senior Citizens can best be illustrated by a recent tragedy in New York City. After the second assault in a matter of weeks, an elderly couple laid out their best clothes for the funeral. Then they wrote a farewell note: "We don't want to live in fear any more," and committed suicide.

Nor were they alone in their terror. National surveys indicate that fear of violent attack has become the *major* concern of the elderly. To combat the spate of crime against the aged—particularly in decaying urban neighborhoods—police and community service groups have at last mobilized. A wide number of programs are currently being tested; the goals vary from education in preventive measures to escort service on trips to the supermarket. Unfortunately, however well-intentioned, such programs will never entirely solve the problem. There simply aren't enough policemen or concerned volunteers to "ride shotgun" for all of the nation's elderly. Thus, like other Americans, our Senior Citizens must ultimately come to the realization that individual safety remains a matter of personal responsiblity.

So how can the elderly protect themselves? Especially against young, streetwise punks whose agility and greater strength provide a distinct advantage. It's a sticky question, one that each Senior Citizen must resolve personally, based on physical condition and the mental willingness to resist. Yet it is *not* an insurmountable problem, and for those determined to defend themselves, there are several options worthy of consideration.

1. *Home Precautions*
   A stout bar-lock will generally discourage even the most experienced burglar. Similarly, a heavy-duty safety chain will allow you to open the door a crack and verify who rang your doorbell. Of course, a peephole device in the door is even better, and common sense is the greatest protection of all. If someone rings the doorbell, *never* take him at face value. If he claims to be a salesman, tell him to get lost. If he claims to be a serviceman of some sort, ask for his superior's name and tell him to wait while you phone to confirm his identity. If he acts peculiar, or attempts to evade legitimate questions, simply slam the door, bolt it, and immediately phone the police. Better a false alarm than the risk of violence. But if he somehow forces his way into your home, then you must consider an altogether different alternative.

2. *Home Alarms and Weapons*
   Every Senior Citizen should have a *very loud* intruder alarm installed in his home. And if the law allows it, a firearm of some description (preferably a shotgun) should be kept handy. Then, whether a burglar sneaks into your home or an intruder

forces his way inside, there's every likelihood the alarm will frighten him off. In the event he's armed—and doesn't run—then a weapon might very well save your life. As a case in point, my parents are retired and live in an area plagued with burglars. Their house is wired throughout with an intruder alarm system, and my father sleeps with a pistol on the bedside table. The pistol is an automatic, loaded with hollow-point bullets; both my mother and father know how to fire it; and neither of them would have any compunctions about using it if confronted with an armed intruder. To paraphrase the old adage, protection starts at home!

3. *Outside the Home*

If at all possible, *never* travel alone. Don't even walk from your apartment to the elevator by yourself unless there's no alternative. Instead, organize your neighbors and band together for errands and shopping trips. There is very definitely strength in numbers—collective security—and street punks are hesitant to attack a group of people. They much prefer a lone victim, caught unaware and defenseless in some isolated spot. So map out your shopping trips or social visits in advance; know every street and dark alley in your neighborhood; take the safest route, even if it's the longest route. Whenever possible, plan your outside activities for those times of day when the streets are crowded with people. If you must travel at night, then stay on well-lighted streets, avoid the shadows and never linger in hallways. And always go with a group. Start ringing doorbells today. Get to know your neighbors! Organize for mutual protection, and create a deterrent effect by sheer weight of numbers. Remember, a street punk is essentially a predator and, given a choice, he'll always attack the weak and the unwary. Don't give him a choice! Travel in groups, and the odds are he'll look elsewhere for a victim.

4. *Physical Resistance*
There can be no hard and fast rule for Senior Citizens confronted with street violence. I have a friend, age 71, who performs manual labor every day and has the constitution of an ox. Moreover, he's one tough sonovabitch, and, personally, I'd hate to tangle with him in a streetfight. And certain ladies are equally fierce. Not long ago an elderly woman in New York routed two purse-snatching hoodlums—with a *very* long hatpin! On the other hand, an elderly person may be infirm or simply incapable of physical defense. So the choice between resistance and surrender depends solely on the individual. If age has affected your strength and coordination, then give the mugger your money and get clear of him as rapidly as possible. If he attacks, and you're unable to run, then fall to the sidewalk and assume the fetal position. Cover your head with your arms and protect your stomach with your knees—and scream like a banshee! Unless he's a psycho, your passive manner and those *bloody murder* screams will usually encourage him to depart the scene. Perhaps you'll get kicked and pummeled, but what he really wants is your money, so let him have it and hope for the best.

If you intend to fight back, then never forget that you might very well be fighting for your life. True weapons are generally illegal in any city or town—assuming you mean to obey the letter of the law—yet any weapon is better than no weapon at all for an elderly person. One very sophisticated lady I know carries a jackknife, and when she's alone she carries it with the blade opened and ready for business. But the decision to use a weapon—hat-pin, umbrella, or whatever—is always risky. It could provoke the assailant, rather than disable him, and result in greater violence. The thought has even grimmer overtones if you're alone and faced by a gang of street thugs. In the final analysis, you must decide for yourself. And be realistic. Base the decision on your physical condition, your ability with the weapon at hand, and a lightning evaluation of your assailant's intent. Sometimes it's simply better to comply with his demands, especially if he's forty years younger and built like a gorilla.

Then again, if he threatens your life rather than your pocketbook, you really have no choice. Senior Citizen or not, you have to do the best you can. And in that situation, do it with all the savagery at your command. You'll never get a second chance.

THE DO AND DON'T CHECKLIST

You will never entirely eliminate the risk of being burglarized. Adequate locks, alarm systems and watchdogs represent major safeguards and deserve serious consideration. But even then, there are certain precautionary measures that will further reduce the hazard. Basically, these are measures which require little more than common sense and foresight. Yet all of them will contribute substantially to the protection of your family and your home.

Do work out a reciprocal arrangement with a neighbor regarding normal daily observation and increased vigilance when you're out of town. Have him and/or her keep a lookout for "daylight" thieves on a regular basis, and periodically check around the house when you're away. If you can afford it, install an automatic timing device to turn lights on and off at intervals. It gives the impression that the house is occupied and, along with an alarm system, will generally discourage the average burglar.

Do install extension phones, particularly in the bedroom. If you need to call the police in the middle of the night, a single phone at the other end of the house would be damned risky. Since the cost of one or more extensions is negligible, it's really "penny foolish" not to give yourself that added edge during a crisis. To be very certain, have a separate line installed in the bedroom. A tricky burglar will take the downstairs phone off the hook, which renders *all* extensions inoperable. Think it over. That bedside phone might very well save your life.

Do complete a detailed inventory of all valuable items in the house. Record the cost, a full description and, where applicable, the serial numbers. Without an itemized inventory, there is every likelihood that you *will not* recover the cost of stolen property from your insurance company. Positive identification is also necessary in the event the police stumble across your color TV or silverware. Unless you have proof of ownership, you'll find city hall can be very slow and very unsympathetic.

Do train all family members in the procedure to be followed during an emergency. Drill them periodically, with wailing burglar alarm and barking dog, so that it becomes a conditioned response. Adults and responsible teen-agers should be trained in the use of weapons and emergency phone procedure; small children should be *taught* to stay in bed and keep their mouths shut until the crisis has passed. By way of example, my wife can control the dog, operate the alarm system, and fire every weapon in the house with admirable results. In a clutch, she also wields a very wicked knife. So if an intruder gets past the alarm and the dog—and me—he's still got one helluva battle on his hands.

Don't rely totally on neighborhood block patrols or private security organizations. If you do, then you've forfeited responsibility for the protection of your home and family. Eventually, you will develop a false sense of security and become careless. Of equal significance, the burglar/rapist/thief is no dummy. He'll simply await an opportune moment and then execute a quick ripoff. I have friends in New York who live between Fifth Avenue and Madison, and own a business establishment on the corner. With crime rampant, the neighborhood organized and hired a security officer to patrol that *one* block during the night. In a six-month period, my friends were burglarized, the store safe was cracked, and their car was stolen off the street. All while the uniformed officer was making his rounds. It was a classic example of underestimating the enemy. And paying double for the experience.

Don't publicize the fact that your house is unoccupied. When you go on vacation, or even a short trip, take rudimentary precautions. In the summer, arrange to have the lawn mowed at regular intervals. Don't allow newspapers or mail to accumulate on the porch. In winter months, arrange for snow removal, and have a neighbor pull in and out of the driveway to give it a "lived in" appearance. Don't fully close the curtains, or leave a yard light burning night and day. And above all, don't announce your vacation plans in the society page. To a burglar, it's no less than an engraved invitation. So stay mum and make sure your house looks *very* normal while you're gone.

Don't broadcast the extent and value of your possessions. Antiques, jewelry, firearms and works of art draw thieves like the proverbial bear to honey. If it becomes common knowledge that your house is a repository of valuable property, then you can shortly expect the burglars. And they'll come in swarms! Or worse, armed robbers will pay you a surprise visit—the kind that plan a caper with military precision and leave no witnesses to link them to the job. Moreover, you're vulnerable no matter where you live. A friend, whose house is located in a remote mountain village, has one of the finest Winchester collections in America. But he made the mistake of publicizing the fact at gun shows, and then compounded the situation by openly displaying his rifles to the public. After several nasty incidents, he now stores the collection in a concrete vault beneath his house. These days, if he wants to exhibit his cherished Winchesters, he has to escort visitors to a lonely underground crypt. His experience with thieves is hardly unique, so take heed. If you own *anything* of intrinsic value, and allow it to become common knowledge, then you do so at your own peril.

Don't depend on your neighbors when an emergency arises. Perhaps they will come to your aid in the event of screams and barking dogs and gunshots.

Then again, perhaps they won't. These days, all too many people believe it's wiser—for them—not to get involved. The classic example, of course, occurred in New York. Kitty Genovese was slowly butchered by a psychotic while thirty-eight neighbors listened—and watched! None came to her rescue; not one was even willing to phone the police. So don't depend on others—neighbors or police—when your home and family are threatened. Depend instead on yourself. Odds are it's the only thing that will save your life.

THE LAST RESORT

You awake.

Out of a misty sleep you hear creaks and unnatural sounds. Cabinets and drawers are cautiously being opened. Very cautiously! Suddenly you wish you had installed that burglar alarm or bought a killer attack dog. But you didn't, and there's someone in the house, so it's make do with what you've got.

Wait!

Don't panic. Fear is a perfectly normal reaction. Take a few deep breaths. Clear your head and steady your nerves. Then lightly touch your wife (make sure it's not *she* who is wandering around the house) and force yourself to lie there and listen. Don't bound out of bed and rush off half-cocked. And above all, don't switch on the bedside lamp. It will destroy your night vision and leave you nakedly vulnerable. Blind as a bat, yet a highly visible target.

Put your senses to work. Close your eyes and relax. Concentrate on those sounds. *Listen!* Isolate the direction and location of the noise. Be very sure you've got it pinpointed before you move. Now gently awaken your wife and whisper a warning. While she calls the police on the bedside phone, ease quietly out of bed and load your stubby scattergun. Then collect that flashlight off the nightstand; have your wife follow behind with her hand on your shoulder, and make your way in the dark to the children's bedroom.

There you have a choice.

Either you wait for the police or you go after the burglar. But you can never *assume* an intruder will hightail it out of the house if you confront him. That could get you killed! So unless you're mentally confident of defending yourself—using deadly force—then step into the children's bedroom and lock the door. Now the family is sequestered in one spot, and if the burglar attempts to bust down the door, you have every right to use the shotgun.

On the other hand, perhaps you believe every man has a moral obligation to defend home and family. Or perhaps your house is in a remote area, and you know the police will never arrive in time. Or maybe you just don't buy the idea of passive submission. Perhaps it's not in your blood to hide and do nothing while the sanctity of your home is violated. So you decide to go after him.

Now it ceases to be idle theory. You're playing for keeps. Leave your wife and kids locked in the bedroom. It is hoped she has a gun of her own and knows how to use it, if the situation demands. If not, and you don't come back, it could place them in jeopardy.

Be that as it may, you're still resolved to go after him. Stalking a night prowler, of course, calls for *zero* mistakes. So it's time to take first things first. Grip the flashlight and forepart of the shotgun in your left hand; snuggle the butt between your elbow and right side; and make damn sure you're barefooted. Now ghost silently through the house, slowly and cautiously, relying on instinct to guide you around obstacles. *Do not alert the intruder to the fact that you're awake!*

Take your time and catfoot every step of the way. In the dark, noise is a killer—literally—so use your knowledge of the house to avoid bumping into anything. Proceed quietly and gingerly toward the direction of *his* sounds. If the house suddenly goes silent, then pause and wait him out. Sooner or later he has to move, and the noise will betray his position. Surprise is your principal ally, and stealth has no substitute. It's a game of hide and seek, and the loser generally gets blown away. But the intruder is on unfamiliar turf. You're in your own home, and you know the layout. Think ahead! Visualize chairs and creaky floorboards and anything that might telegraph your movements. So long as you don't blunder, you've got the edge. The tactical advantage.

Use it. Keep your wits and *think!*

However long it takes, don't rush. You have to assume he's armed, and unwarranted haste could get the wrong man killed. Stay loose and prepare yourself emotionally to go the limit. He might be waiting with a knife or a sharpened screwdriver. Or worse, he might have a gun. You won't know for certain until you find him. But that's too late. So don't get careless and don't take anything for granted.

Presume he's armed and potentially homicidal. Fully prepared to kill in order to avoid being caught. And since it's your house, then it's *you* he's prepared to kill.

If he's not armed, consider it your lucky night. Yet it could happen, and if it does, you only get one chance. There won't be time for talk or hesitation or warning shots. Not if he's armed. There will merely be a split-second—an instant of judgment—before you're forced to take action.

It's called the last resort.

Unless he's alerted, of course, you'll find him before he finds you. Not even burglars can see in the dark. So look for a small penlight, usually rose-lensed, and keep your ears tuned to his movements. Isolate the room he's in and pad silently to the doorway. Then halt where you have a clear angle of fire. Wait till you're absolutely certain of his position and press the button on your flashlight. Fix him in the beam and level the shotgun on his belt buckle. Now it's his move and your choice, and there's no turning back. All of which boils down to the man and the moment and a single premise.

Save your life!

HAND-TO-HAND COMBAT

Yea, though I walk through the valley of the shadow of death, I will fear no evil; for I am the meanest sonovabitch in the valley.
—Anonymous

Assault and Battery is an Old and Honored Custom

ANCIENT civilizations, both Oriental and Occidental, approached close-quarters combat with a sort of savage fervor. In the western hemisphere, the Greeks were perhaps the first to organize combat into a sporting event. Having refined wrestling to a near science, they went on to slugfests in which iron spikes were strapped to the fists. Not to be outdone, the Romans institutionalized mayhem and gave the world gladiators, who dutifully mangled one another with a bizarre array of weapons. The Oriental branch of the family, meanwhile, perfected its own inscrutable method of rendering an antagonist insensible. Ultimately the most widely practiced offshoot of this discipline came to be known as karate. Somewhat more pragmatic than their Western cousins, the Orientals have maintained to the present day a noticeably keener sense of survival. Karate embraces a quasi-religious spirit, but it also advocates striking or kicking to any part of an adversary's anatomy, which establishes a rather neat line of demarcation between idealism and realism.

Perhaps of greater consequence, we find in the Eastern attitude toward the martial arts an affirmation of yet an older truth. *Mankind has an enduring penchant for violence.* Unhappily, there are predators among us, and it's in the nature of the beast to prey on his fellows. So turning the other cheek will usually get you a black eye.

All things considered, then, it seems we have come full circle. The streets of America are no less hazardous than the cobblestone byways of ancient civilizations. Instead of brigands and footpads, we have muggers and armed robbers, and drug addicts often turned psycho. By any name, however, one stark fact is inescapable. Since our ancestors swung down out of the trees, the instincts of certain men remain remarkably unaltered. If anything, the predators who stalk modern streets have grown more daring with time, and considerably more vicious. And why not? Their prey is unarmed for the most part and, if apprehended, the courts turn them loose with little more than a slap on the wrist. Only human predators have it so good; in other jungles the law of nature exacts retribution even on the hunter. Yet, for the peaceful citizen, the hazard factor has increased by quantum leaps. Hundreds of thousands of men and women have already learned the lesson the hard way. The individual who walks the street *unarmed* had best prepare to defend himself in hand-to-hand combat. It's only a matter of time.

Still, however harsh it sounds, we cannot entirely absolve ourselves of fault. *The average American has become a softy as regards his mental outlook on what constitutes a streetfight.* Decades of misguided altruism have promulgated the virtues of fair play and sportsmanship. Worse, we've been taught the somewhat dubious adage, "It's how you play the game that counts, not whether you win or lose." Over the generations, our search for loftier ideals has steadily eroded the *instinct* to defend oneself by whatever means necessary. To a large extent, it has sapped the individual of all volition to resist an assailant who threatens either property or physical harm. It's an insidious philosophy, manifested in actions which contradict our every urge for survival. We see it exhibited in the "new" reluctance to strike the first blow, or even worse, to kick an opponent. The average citizen is deeply inhibited about employing such tactics and, as a result, we have become the victims of our own civility. Not all of us—perhaps not you—but to such an extent that it's become our national syndrome.

Strong stuff? Offensive to your ear? You bet it is! But it's also the truth. If you think otherwise, then pause and reflect a moment. Visualize yourself kicking a mugger in the teeth while he's flat on his back. Now be honest! Odds are you couldn't bring yourself to do it. Not while he's down. If so, then you're in real trouble. You have subverted all the defensive mechanisms nature gave you, and on the streets of America today, you're a prime candidate for the meat wagon. That mugger can and will get up off the sidewalk and kill you. It happens every day, like clockwork. So don't wait for Providence or the beat cop to save you. Save yourself! Keep reading, and you'll discover that being a good guy doesn't necessarily mean you're Mr. Clean.

To most Americans, it has become all but impossible to separate the rules of boxing from the older laws governing a streetfight. Obviously, one bears no relationship whatever to the other, yet millions of people remain afflicted with those loftier ideals. In an alley or on a dark street, however, survival remains the primeval law of man. When the fight ends, the only thing that counts is who won and who lost; muggers and rapists display a notable lack of appreciation for "the way the game is played." Sportsmanship and fair play, viewed from their twisted psyches, merely represent a limitation which the law-abiding citizen imposes on himself. Nothing if not practical, the criminal relies instead on tactics eminently suited to streetfighting. So the wise man quickly adapts, and learns to play the game by the other fellow's rules. Since the mugger/rapist has no inhibitions concerning *dirty fighting,* then the name of that particular game becomes who can do the most damage in the least amount of time. On the street there are no options: one's schoolboy honor must be momentarily suspended. Once the fight becomes imminent, the prudent individual will strike first and ensure by whatever means necessary that his assailant is neutralized. Down and out and done for.

Years ago, my father gave me a sage piece of advice. Our ranch was located in western cow country, where kicking and boot stomping and eye gouging were accepted expedients in a Saturday night brawl. So at an early age he instructed me that anything goes in a fight—the object was to win—even if it meant clobbering your opponent with an axe handle. The wisdom of his advice was indelibly etched on my mind only a short time later. I was sitting astraddle another fellow, pounding the stuffing out of him and having myself a helluva good workout. Suddenly he grabbed a fist-sized rock and planted it (with indisputable results) squarely between my eyes. Once coldcocked, twice wary—to paraphrase the old maxim—for I still carry the scar. In several altercations over ensuing years, the lesson came in very handy. It's quicker, neater and far less damaging to your own constitution to strike first with whatever it takes to get the job done.

All too many men involved in a streetfight fall victim to the exaggerated power of their own fist. Beguiled by television's fantasyland, where the hero *always* decks his adversary with one punch, the homeowner naturally assumes it's as easy as it looks. Only when it's too late—that is, when he's lying on the ground having his features rearranged—does he discover that a one-punch knockout is highly improbable. In fact, the majority of streetfights begin and end without a knockout; seldom is anyone decked by a blow of the fist. If you doubt the truth of that statement, then consider a statistical absolute. In the history of the ring, only a handful of *professional boxers* have been able to compile an impressive knockout record.

To anyone who has been involved in streetfights, it is readily apparent that the opening blow rarely puts an opponent on ice. Worse, a mugger fully expects that you—Mr. Clean—will defend yourself with your fists. He also knows that whatever defensive ability you possess is generally limited to an "armchair" knowledge of boxing. Further, and all the more disillusioning, he knows that few men have either the physical power or the training to take out an antagonist with one punch. So he has lots of street savvy, and he's not in the least frightened by the thunderbolt in your right arm.

Police blotters bear witness to the fact that men who rely on their fists are often crippled—even killed—by an assailant schooled in the practical value of dirty fighting. The average citizen would do well to remember that his opponent's head is considerably harder than his own fist; the odds against ending the fight with one or two punches are virtually astronomical. While you might connect with a couple of haymakers to the jaw, your streetwise assailant will end the fracas with a low blow or a swift kick where it hurts most.

Quite obviously, then, something more than the doubled fist is required in a streetfight. Sportsmanlike inhibitions will merely get you crippled or maimed. Or worse. But perhaps you're still not convinced. Maybe you participated in the Golden Gloves, or the Armed Forces boxing program, and rate yourself a scrappy, toe-to-toe slugger. So let's consider another factor: stamina. On the street or in the ring, if you intend to swap punches then you need endurance. Without it, that thunderbolt right cross quickly becomes a marshmallow love tap. To illustrate the point, assess yourself with the quiz below, and briefly compare the you of *today* with the you of *yesterday*.

1. Can you jog a mile without your lungs collapsing and your legs turning to jelly?

2. Can you do 25 full push-ups without muscle spasms in your arms and shoulders?

3. Can you do 25 sit-ups without spraining your sacroiliac?

4. Can you do 25 deep kneebends without your thighs turning to mush?

5. Can you touch your toes, without bending your knees, or does that spare tire halt you around belt level?

An emphatic "yes" to *all* of the above qualifies you for a fast *sixty seconds* of toe-to-toe action. An honest "no" to *any* of the above qualifies you for one helluva beating in a streetfight. Assuming, of course, that you still intend to use your fists. If not, then there are other ways. Fast and practical, perhaps a bit unorthodox, and dirty as hell. Not the gutter tactics your assailant will use, but something better. And very final

Before proceeding further, perhaps a moment's reflection is in order. Since fisticuffs are highly impractical—especially for women—suppose we consider the alternative that immediately springs to mind. Karate. Kung Fu. The martial arts of the Orient.

Within the last decade, karate has captured the imagination of thousands of men and women throughout America. Currently, there are more than 4000 karate schools across the country; students are taught a repertoire of tricks (developed by Zen Buddhists) to thwart attack and deliver instant retaliation. Undoubtedly, those who progress through the eight levels of proficiency—the coveted black belt—make formidable opponents indeed. Let's face it, anyone who can shatter concrete blocks with "*kara* (empty) *te* (hand)" hardly ranks as a creampuff. The individual willing to spend months conditioning his body, and up to three years attaining adequate skills, can walk the streets almost as safely as if he had a loaded gun strapped to his hip.

Unfortunately, most Americans have neither the time nor the inclination to subject themselves to the training regimen and physical demands of karate. Moreover, from a statistical standpoint, the prospects appear bleak for the average student. Only a small percentage of those enrolled ever qualify for the black belt. In the case of women, it's a chancey proposition at best. The owner of a noted karate school admitted that less than one-third of the women who enter training attain the necessary skills to defend themselves. Thus, it appears that the individual—man or woman—would benefit by a system of self-defense that relies on instinct and natural cunning rather than training; a method that employs swift, decisive blows, yet requires neither physical conditioning nor a daily program of combat practice.

One last thought: Karate is a deadly science, unexcelled by any known form of unarmed self-defense. If you have the time and the mental discipline required, then enroll today and begin working toward that black belt. But if you haven't the proper motivation—or lack the wherewithal—then absorb every detail of the pages to follow. It could very well save your life.

The hands are marvelous tools, designed by nature to perform an infinite variety of tasks. Properly utilized, they also become lethal weapons. However, the effect of any blow is in direct ratio to the *function* of the target. Hit a man on the arm and he might wince. Plant your knuckles in his windpipe and it's lights out. So there we have the cardinal rule of hand-to-hand combat. ***Strike to vital targets!*** Concentrate on targets that will interrupt *vital* body functions and instantly neutralize your assailant.

Throughout man's odyssey of close-quarters combat he has discovered many sensitive and inviting targets. But none seem quite so tempting, or possess that sense of swift finality, as the throat. In fact, the throat and/or neck is the *prime* target in a streetfight. It provides ready access to various nerves and blood vessels; if struck with precision, your assailant will be disabled immediately, perhaps permanently. The blow familiar to everyone, of course, is the rabbit punch or karate chop to the outside base of the neck. However, to be effective, this blow must be executed with great force. Otherwise the carotid artery will not undergo sufficient damage to induce shock and momentary blackout.

Perhaps the most vulnerable target, and certainly the one least anticipated by your assailant, is the Adam's apple. Quite prominent on men, it is formed by the largest cartilage of the larynx, which controls both the vocal cords and the windpipe. When struck squarely, the larynx contracts with a death-grip spasm. The windpipe is instantly sealed by shattered cartilage and mucus, denying air to the lungs. In addition to the gagging effect created by starved lungs, the pain in the throat is so excruciating as to be indescribable.

It requires little imagination to visualize the sense of terror experienced by a man subjected to such an attack. If you have any doubt as to the effect of a crushed larynx, then simply allow someone—preferably a friend—to flip your Adam's apple with a forceful rap of the middle finger. One demonstration will generally persuade even the broadest skeptic. So fix the target in your mind! Never forget that it's the optimum weapon in your arsenal of tricks. *To neutralize an assailant instantly, direct your blow to the larynx!*

The point cannot be overstressed. Strike at the Adam's apple and your advantage automatically doubles. First, the advantage of surprise. Since your assailant anticipates a conventional defense, he will be caught off guard by a totally unexpected blow to the throat. Second, the advantage of avoiding a prolonged fight. Crush the larynx, and your assailant will be taken out of action on the spot. Alone and unarmed, that's no small consideration when you're confronted by a larger adversary or an experienced streetfighter. So surprise and a quick end to the fight represent two excellent reasons for adopting this particular tactic. However, a word of caution. If the blow is delivered full strength, then the probability exists that it will produce a lethal effect.

The illustration in *Fig. 1* depicts a direct strike to the Adam's apple. Standing face-to-face with your assailant, the blow should be delivered with the knuckles formed by folding your fingers back to the second joint. Without warning, step forward on your left foot; thrust *upward*

Figure 1(A).

with the force of your right arm and shoulder, and direct your blow slightly above the base of the throat *(A)*. If you strike a bit low, don't worry. The skidding force of the blow will still jam your knuckles upward into the larynx. Standing sideways to your assailant, the Adam's apple becomes somewhat less accessible. In that event, deliver a karate chop with the outside edge of your hand. Crouch and swing toward your assailant to create maximum force; sweep your arm up and backward on a *short* arc; strike with the edge of your hand slightly above the base of the throat. *NOTE:* The position of your assailant will dictate which blow should be employed. However, either of these blows must be delivered with an *upward* motion. Otherwise you risk hitting the chin or jawbone, which would have little effect on your assailant.

In a streetfight only a saint or a misguided fool would

Figure 1(B).

stop with one blow. Once gained, the advantage must be pressed, *regardless of the effect of the first blow,* until there is not the slightest chance of retaliation. Thus, a blow to the larynx is *always* followed by a full-force kick to the stomach *(B).* Since your assailant's lungs are already starved for oxygen, the stomach kick will compound his problem enormously. With few exceptions, it will end the fight very quickly indeed.

The larynx is the *key* target, especially for women or men of slight stature. It's vulnerable simply because it can be crushed with so little force. Take your assailant by surprise. Once he threatens you, strike first and strike without warning. Hit him squarely in the Adam's apple, and follow it with an enthusiastic kick to the belly. He'll go down, and he'll stay down!

On the other hand, perhaps you won't get a clear shot

Figure 2(A).

Figure 2(B).

at the larynx. Streetfights vary from situation to situation; you may have to adjust your tactics accordingly. The veteran has *several* battle plans, and numerous secondary targets. Wisely, he remains flexible and learns to tailor the opening blow to fit the situation. Given a choice, go for the larynx. But if your options narrow, then shift sights and take a look at the nose. It has infinite possibilities as a fight-stopper.

Hardly a conventional target, the nose is nonetheless more closely guarded than the throat. Yet it presents an opportunity to end the fight with one blow. Here again, utilize surprise, the unexpected attack! The illustration in *Fig. 2* depicts an attack initiated from a relaxed standing position. Step forward on your left foot; simultaneously throw the weight of your shoulder behind the blow, and strike *upward* with your elbow cocked and locked. Aim low, near the mouth, and slam the butt of your hand into the bottom of your assailant's nose, where it joins the upper lip *(A)*. Always aim a bit low; it's better to strike him in the mouth than to overshoot the nose and hit nothing. Properly executed, this blow will break the nose, jam cartilage back up inside the head and create a wave of pain unlike anything your assailant ever imagined possible. Once again, a word of caution. Delivered with excessive force, the probable result of this blow would be lethal. Bone and cartilage driven upward into the brain often have a terminal effect.

To gain maximum surprise, you should stand casually, with arms hanging loosely at your sides. Then simply step forward—no warning—and slam upward with your right hand. Of course, the use of this attack presumes that you have been threatened with bodily harm. Therefore the end result is justified.

But don't stop now! Press your advantage. Without hesitation, while your assailant clutches his shattered nose, swing your right leg upward and deliver a full-force knee to the groin *(B)*. The nose slam and groin blow employed in tandem will generally tranquilize anything short of an adult gorilla. Since the attack requires speed and nerve—rather than great physical strength—it can be executed very effectively by women.

A brief aside to illustrate the value of speed and nerve in a hostile situation. Some years ago a fellow I know (of average height and medium build) was confronted by a street gang in the lobby of a theater. When push came to shove—the four toughs had him backed up against a wall—he laid out the leader with a quick hand-slam to the nose. Blood splattered in every direction, and the impact of the blow had a singular effect on the rest of the gang. They decided to forego the contest, and hastily carted their "pug-nosed" commander to the nearest hospital. Under the circumstances, the fellow involved had no choice. He would have taken a beating—or worse—had he hesitated. By acting decisively, he narrowed the odds; by neutralizing the gang leader, he convinced the other members to back off. The moral: don't curse your luck and pray for deliverance. Strike first and strike fast, and do maximum damage with that opening blow.

On occasion, the action in hand-to-hand combat develops so quickly that you haven't the time to deliver a crippling blow. This is particularly true when you're jumped by an assailant who attacks rather than threatens. But even then, you can still employ the element of surprise and strike where least expected.

Perhaps the weakest spot on the American physique of today is the soft underbelly of the stomach. Starchy food and a taste for beer have expanded the stomach into a flabby roll that fairly invites attack. Yet the majority of men engaged in a streetfight still expect to be struck in the face. Especially the mugger/rapist who has selected Mr. Clean (or Ms. Clean) as his next victim. With few exceptions, they are stunned breathless (literally) when the

Figure 3(A).

first blow is directed instead to the tub-o'-guts below their waistline.

The illustration in *Fig. 3* depicts a closed-fist punch directed to the tender underbelly *(A).* The move is executed by stepping forward on your left foot and delivering the blow in an uppercut manner below the beltline. Usually an assailant will be taken completely unaware: the blow is delivered from a relaxed standing position and strikes where least expected. *NOTE:* While a seasoned streetfighter *always* guards against a kick to the groin, he rarely anticipates that the *opening blow* will be a low blow with the fist.

Executed swiftly, the blow will empty an assailant's lungs and leave him gasping for breath. With spasms in his gut and a case of the dry heaves, he's momentarily defenseless. Now is the time to finish him off!

Figure 3(B).

The low blow will generally double your assailant over and cause him to clutch his belly. With your left leg still extended, simply swing your right knee up and plant it in his face *(B)*. The move becomes all the more potent if you grab his hair with both hands; jerk his head down and forward; and slam your knee upward to connect with his descending face. His downward momentum impacted on the upward velocity of your knee is guaranteed to produce results. The force of these blows—delivered with the *wham! wham!* of a trip hammer—will normally put an assailant down and out. If he does attempt to rise, then buy yourself a little insurance. Kick him in the teeth and bounce his head off the sidewalk. In the argot of the street, that's that!

Another secondary target is the heart. Less vulnerable

Figure 4(A).

than either the larynx or the nose, it is nonetheless an unexpected attack zone and capitalizes on the element of surprise. Widely employed in Oriental defense techniques, a blow to the heart will often paralyze an assailant and leave him virtually helpless. To be effective, however, the blow must be delivered with great force. The mass of bone and muscle surrounding the heart forms a solid barrier; considerable power is required to impact the breastbone and transmit shock to the heart itself. But it can be done—by any man or woman of average strength—and the result is highly conclusive. In fact, if the breastbone is splintered and penetrates the heart, the effect then becomes lethal.

The illustration in *Fig. 4* depicts an attack to the heart. The initial blow can be delivered from a casual standing

Figure 4(B).

position (to achieve surprise), or any time during the fight when your assailant is at arm's length. Step forward on your left foot; simultaneously throw the weight of your shoulder behind your arm; direct an *upward* blow to the breastbone *(A)*. The blow is delivered with the butt of your hand (heel of the palm); the breastbone (or sternum) is the junction formed by the *top* of each rib cage and the *bottom* bones of the chest. Explore your own chest and locate the triangular junction of the breastbone; fix it in your mind and always deliver the blow to that *exact* spot. Properly executed, the blow will induce paralysis and/or loss of consciousness.

However, it cannot be overstressed that the shock effect of a heart punch is often momentary and must be reinforced immediately by a second blow. The nearest target, since your left leg and right arm are already extended, is the Adam's apple. Merely pull your arm back a few inches and ram your knuckles *upward* into the larynx *(B)*. An alternative, depending on the situation, would be to kick or knee your assailant in the groin/stomach area.

An attack to the heart should *never* be attempted at close range (less than arm's length) since it is difficult to generate sufficient power with a short punch. Still, the heart/larynx attack, executed with full force, will neutralize your assailant on the instant. So don't hesitate to use it, but make sure you put every ounce of energy you possess behind that opening blow.

The hands are damaging weapons when utilized properly. Individuals of slight stature—both men and women—can immobilize a mugger/rapist of greater physical strength if a *vital* blow is combined with the element of surprise. The prime essentials are the determination to defend yourself and the nerve to strike the first blow when threatened. Never allow an assailant to gain the initiative; hesitation can get you killed. Given the slightest opportunity, strike first! Use whatever tactics necessary to win a streetfight; your actions are justified by hostile threats and/or overt assault. Unless you're built like an NFL linebacker, forget your fists and conventional blows to the head. Even then, if you've never before knocked a man out with one punch, forget it! Go for the throat, deliver a solid jab to the Adam's apple. That takes all the steam out of your assailant, and it settles the argument in a highly persuasive manner.

If most Americans are inhibited about crushing an assailant's larynx, then the thought of kicking him must induce something akin to panic. Yet, for a sure-fire fight-stopper, nothing beats an enthusiastic kick to some delicate portion of the anatomy. Certainly, your assailant has no qualms about using his feet; to test the statement, merely stand in an exposed position when accosted by a mugger. The feet are potent weapons, and any veteran streetfighter considers the swift kick his dynamite tactic. So unless you plan on sprinting to safety, then shed those inhibitions and mentally condition yourself to kick. It's ugly, and perhaps you'll be revolted, but it may very well save your life.

Inexperienced or seasoned, anyone involved in a streetfight *expects* a kick to the groin. In fact, a veteran will enter an engagement standing at a slight angle to his opponent. Thus, he's prepared, by turning his hip slightly, to deflect a kick to vital organs. So a wily individual, particularly if he radiates that Mr. Clean innocence, can outsmart his streetwise assailant. Launch the kick—fake him into turning sideways—then kick him squarely in the *kneecap.* Seldom if ever does anyone anticipate a kick to the knee, and yet it's a very accessible part of the body. Those who have experienced the sensation recall quite vividly that it paralyzed their entire leg. Shock and surprise, along with intense pain, will also freeze your assailant's reaction time. Then he's a sitting duck—albeit hopping on one leg—for the final blow of the fight.

The illustration in *Fig. 5* depicts a kick delivered from the relaxed standing position. Anticipating a kick to the groin, the savvy streetfighter turned his hip and was struck instead on the kneecap *(A).* The situation, of course, dictates how the kick is executed. In a surprise attack, used as the opening blow, the kick must be delivered with the toe of the shoe. Only then will an assailant be suckered into protecting his groin and inadvertently exposing his knee. However, in the midst of a fight, particularly when an assailant rushes you, the kick should be delivered sideways, with the bottom of the shoe. To execute the side kick, raise your foot knee high and simultaneously pivot ninety degrees on the other foot. Then kick out with the full force of your leg, directly into the front of the knee. Greater power is generated with the side kick; it's not at all uncommon to shatter an opponent's kneecap and literally cripple him for life.

Figure 5(A).

Figure 5(B).

The spontaneous reaction of anyone kicked in the knee is to double over, grabbing his leg. That's the exact moment you follow through with an upward hand-slam to the nose *(B)*. The assailant's forward momentum will drive him full tilt into the upward impact of the blow. Normally, that ends the fight without further exertion. If it appears necessary, however, simply cock your arm to the left and sweep backwards with a side-neck chop into the larynx. On top of the kick and the nose job, this *coup de grâce* will take the fight out of anything that walks on its hind legs. I once observed a full-blooded Cherokee bouncer tame an unruly rodeo champion in just this manner. The broncbuster looked as though he'd been mauled by a grizzly bear; upon being released from the hospital, he spent several months recuperating. Next year, when the rodeo came to town, he went out of his way to avoid that particular honky-tonk.

While a kick to the groin is *always* anticipated, it's often possible to knee an assailant between the legs. Delivered full-force, it's a devastating blow. Generally, the opportunity occurs when you're grappling hand-to-hand with your assailant. Even then, he's on guard against the knee-to-groin tactic; your chances are vastly improved if you divert his attention. Bite him! Stick a thumb in his eye! Butt upward with your head! Use any ruse that fits the situation. Then slam your knee into his crotch.

Anyone kneed in the groin will double up with violent contractions, and most men vomit like a sick child. In fact, at that point, your assailant is helpless as a baby. So when his body slumps forward, simply step back and let him have a hand-slam straight up the schnozz. It's not easily done, but if you pull it off, then the fight's over. A knee in the crotch, topped off by a squashed nose, will deflate any man's balloon. Big or small, short or tall, they all fall when you bust their gonads.

Which brings us to the tactic that advocates of fair play will find absolutely loathsome. That holiest of all taboos: kicking an opponent when he's down. A mugger obeys neither conscience nor rules, especially if he's a drug addict in need of a fix. Once he gets *you* down, he'll stomp you into a puddle merely as a matter of form. So if you're accosted on the street, bear in mind that it's not a game. You're on his turf, and the only law he understands is dog-eat-dog. It's a sad commentary on the human condition, but it's nonetheless true. Ignore it at your own peril. Come to grips with it mentally and it save could your life.

The overriding consideration, of course, is to minimize further risk once you gain the advantage. If you knock an assailant to the ground, but fail to finish him off, then his infuriated mental state makes him all the more dangerous. The man who can regain his feet after absorbing the blows and kicks previously described is an adversary so formidable as to warrant either extreme action or extreme caution. Your choice, then, is quite simple: either finish the job or run like hell!

The pragmatic individual will opt to settle the matter with dispatch. While he might harbor reservations about gutter tactics, he's vastly more concerned with his own survival. And rightly so. Thus he will close on a downed *but still dangerous* assailant and kick him in the jaw. The kick is directed to the jaw instead of the temple or upper head; the purpose is to render your assailant unconscious rather than deliver a lethal blow. Without hesitation, you must then guarantee that he's drained of the will to fight. Drive the air from his lungs with a kick to the ribs or the pit of the stomach.

However repugnant, that's the law of the street. Not a law of your choosing, but the only law applicable if ever you're assaulted. So once you've downed an assailant, don't go squeamish! Ensure by whatever means necessary that he doesn't rise until the police arrive.

Thus far we have discussed situations in which you detect imminent danger and strike the first blow. Yet there are times when *you* will be taken by surprise. The basic tactics of a mugger/rapist—much preferred to direct confrontation—are stealth and the silent ambush. No threats. No warning. He simply jumps you from a dark alley. Or perhaps he passes you on the street, then whirls and attacks from the rear. Now *he* has the advantage, and you've lost the chance to strike the first blow.

But you haven't lost the chance to retaliate. Not if you keep your head and react quickly. The key to survival now becomes instinct combined with a knowledge of counterattack.

The mugger/rapist employs a variety of arm locks and/or strangleholds to silence his victim. Once attacked, it is imperative that you break loose and *create* the opportunity for counterattack. Your reaction must be instantaneous and violent; the assailant's hold will grow stronger with each passing moment. So the first step is instinct: react within the split-second he grabs you. The second move is counteraction: go for the weak spot and break his hold. The last step is unrestrained aggression: you counterattack simultaneously upon breaking loose. All the blows and kicks previously described are used in any combination that fits the situation. Strike hard and strike fast. Strike to *vital* targets! Seize the initiative and neutralize your assailant while he's off balance.

The illustrations in *Figs. 6–10* depict several attacks favored by the mugger/rapist. Within each sequence are the attack; the escape; the counterattack. Bear in mind, however, that technique alone will never suffice in hand-to-hand combat. It's reaction time and an instinct for the jugular that will ultimately save your life.

Figure 6. His arm locks around your throat in a stranglehold. Instantly butt backwards with your head and squash his nose. Or slump forward, then suddenly throw yourself backward, and bite his forearm. Or rake his shinbone with the heel of your shoe and stomp *hard* on his instep. The moment the arm lock weakens: twist your body to the right; pull down on his wrist and push up on his elbow; and wrench your head clear. Then spin to the left and drive your right fist into his groin. Finish him off with a knee in the face; kicks to the knee; or a jab to larynx. Strike to any target of opportunity, but strike fast!

Figure 7. An alternate escape from the arm lock around your throat. It's tricky and must be executed the instant he grabs you. Grasp his forearm with your left hand and his shoulder (or hair) with your right hand. Simultaneously drop to your right knee; heave forward with your arms; lever him up with your shoulders; and throw him overhead. The moment you let go, jump to your feet; as he attempts to rise, kick him in the back of the head at the base of the skull. Or instead, remain kneeling; jerk his head back with your left hand; and deliver a chop to the larynx with your right hand. Either counterattack will end the fight.

Figure 8. His hand clamps across your mouth from behind. Instantly grab his little finger and jerk down with all your strength. (If he resists, and tries for a stranglehold, then bite his hand as it comes away from your mouth.) Twist the little finger down to waist level; release his hand and pivot on your right foot; snap your right arm back in a short arc and deliver a karate chop to the larynx. Or instead, twist the little finger aside; release his hand and step away on your left foot; then kick back with your right foot to the knee or stomach/groin. Finally, strike to any target of opportunity and put him away.

Figure 9. He grabs your throat in a stranglehold from the front. Immediately jab your fingers into his eyes. If you blind him, so much the better. But the primary goal is to distract him while you slam your knee into his crotch. An alternative is to ram your knuckles into his larynx and then knee him in the groin. If he somehow avoids both the eyes and/or larynx blows, then throw your arms up and out (against the inside of his arms) to break the stranglehold. Simultaneously thrust your knee between his legs. While any of these tactics might very well disable him, don't leave it to chance. Counterattack once you've broken the stranglehold.

Figure 10. His hands are locked around your wrist in an effort to drag you along. Simply lean back against the force of his pull; pivot on your left foot and raise your right leg; then deliver a sideways kick to the kneecap. If he avoids the kick, then *allow* him to jerk you forward and ram the knuckles of your free hand into his larynx. If that fails and he grabs both arms (or pulls you into a bear hug) then literally go for the jugular. Bite him in the side of the neck— as deep as possible— and rip outward with your teeth. The instant he releases you, counterattack with kicks and blows until he's out of the fight.

THE DO AND DON'T CHECKLIST. All streets are dangerous. Once you step outside your home, whether you travel on foot or by car, you have entered a hostile environment. If the statement offends your sensibilities, or has a paranoid ring, then you're kidding no one but yourself. Simply read the evening newspaper or listen to tonight's newscast. All that mugging/rape/robbery/assault/burglary has actually happened. And it happened to people exactly like yourself! Except that the ones you read about chose to ignore reality. Either they weren't capable of defending themselves or else they turned a blind eye to the dangers of the world about them.

Street violence is *not* limited to the ghetto. The mugger/rapist now stalks the well-lighted, affluent streets of America. Ask any cop. He'll tell you that the predators prefer to work respectable neighborhoods. The loot is better and the victims are plentiful. Or if you need further proof, check the latest FBI crime statistics. A trend has developed in recent years. The affluent and the middle-class have fled the cities. And guess what? Crime has skyrocketed in the suburbs and small towns. Which should come as no great surprise. The predators are following you, like wolves tracking the herd. It's all very elemental. Hunters stalk their prey where the grass is green and the herd well fed. In a metaphorical sense, it's merely frightening. In reality, it could cost you all you have, including your life.

So beware and be prepared. It happens every day and it might one day happen to you. Anywhere! Any time!

And then *you* have become a statistic.

On the Road:

Do drive with the doors locked and the windows closed. Street hoodlums, particularly robbers and rapists, are fond of jumping into cars at stop signs or traffic lights. Once he puts a knife to your throat, you could lose it all. Your money, your body, perhaps your life.

Do carry a weapon of some sort in your car. While guns are generally prohibited, there are ways to defend yourself. A baseball bat is very convincing, and it's also legal to carry one in your car. If you're attacked, three feet of ⅜″ logging chain is even more persuasive. However, avoid blows to the head and you will avoid trouble with the law. Instead, fake to the head, then attack the knees, legs and arms. Neutralize your assailant with a busted kneecap and wait for the police to arrive.

Do install a CB radio in your car. Excellent CB units are available at bargain prices, and a woman driving alone couldn't have a better friend. In a crisis, flip to Emergency Channel 9 and you'll have Smokies there within a short while. However, beware of other Good Samaritans. Recently a woman's car stalled and she radioed for help. Two well-dressed types came to the rescue, promptly robbed and raped her, and took off headed that-a-way. So if your car stalls, broadcast on Channel 9, or lacking CB, tie a handkerchief to the aerial. Then lock all doors and wait for Smokey. Or a burly trucker. Both are dependable, and very handy in *any* sort of emergency.

Do choose motels with ***brightly*** lighted parking areas when you're on a trip. Overnight, your car could be stolen or vandalized if it's left in a dark, secluded spot. So remove all valuables from the car and, if necessary, park it near the bright lights at the front of the motel. A short walk next morning is better than waking to find yourself with no wheels at all.

Don't drive in high crime areas or slum districts unless it's absolutely necessary. Your car and *you* are out of place and merely invite attack by street gangs. In a very real sense, you're a foreigner—an outsider—and that makes you fair game. Sadder still, it's open season year round on anyone who looks like an easy mark. So save yourself a lot of grief. Avoid areas where—right or wrong—you're automatically tagged as the enemy.

Don't park your car on dark side streets. Never, under any circumstances, park it in an isolated area. At best, your car might be stripped, vandalized or stolen. At worst, *you* might be robbed, raped or murdered. The risk increases by quantum leaps, so don't expose yourself to needless jeopardy. Choose a well-lighted street, or better yet, choose a parking garage with an attendant. Granted, the charges are high these days, but it might be the best investment you ever made. Life insurance of sorts.

Don't get into your car until you've checked out the back seat. The rule is especially applicable to women, and at night it's a vital precaution. Someone could be crouched on the floorboard—waiting—and then you become a statistic. It happened to friends of mine: the fellow was stabbed and dumped at roadside; the girl was raped repeatedly and never quite recovered. Perhaps it will never happen to you—if you're lucky. But luck is damned capricious, and never to be trusted. So trust yourself instead. Check out the back seat.

Don't give in to that kindly urge and pick up hitchhikers. Perhaps it's a young girl and her innocent-looking boyfriend, so you figure they're harmless. Think again! Not long ago, just such a pair killed one motorist, robbed another and kidnapped a third. I always feel guilty when I whiz past a hitchhiker; as a youngster, I thumbed cross-country, and people everywhere were nice enough to give me a lift. But times have changed. These days, you stop at your own peril, and it might very well be your last stop. So suppress the urge, and keep your foot on the gas pedal.

On the Street:

Do assume that any street, night or day, has the potential for danger. No need to become paranoid, but a healthy dose of skepticism about *everyone* will help you avoid hazardous situations. Stay on well-lighted streets; swing wide around corners and doorway entrances; and skirt *anything* that might be an ambush site for the mugger/rapist. Never take a risky shortcut—especially an alley or a parking lot—and avoid being caught alone in hallways or stairwells. In short, be suspicious and be damned careful.

Do keep your eyes open, and remain constantly aware of everything happening in the near vicinity. Your first line of defense is simple *alertness!* In fact, there's no substitute for a keen eye and the good sense to take evasive action *before* danger threatens. Cross the street or run in the opposite direction if you're approached by someone acting suspicious. It's an obvious expedient, yet it often discourages the mugger/rapist. So stay alert and keep your wits. Once the warning light flashes in your head, use that split-second reprieve to swerve off a collision course. In other words, make yourself scarce. Quickly!

Do carry a self-defense weapon of some sort. Guns and sheath knives are illegal, of course, so that comes down to a matter of personal judgment. Police recommend referee-type whistles or battery-operated sirens, but don't stake your life on such devices. Seldom will the racket attract enough attention to save your from being mugged or worse. Yet you still have the option of a Jackknife or a Folding Hunter. And not long ago, on a trip to New York, I noticed that certain "items" had become quite fashionable. Some people were striding around Manhattan with *very* heavy walking sticks, and others regularly travel the streets at night carrying a golf club. Apparently the thought of a putter upside the head acts as a real deterrent to muggers. It's all a matter of innovation and imagination. Weapons come in various shapes and sizes, some more recognizable than others.

As a last resort, there are several chemical spray type devices on the market. Commonly called "tear gas" guns, these devices come in various shapes and sizes, nearly all suitable for concealment in either purse or coat pocket. Actually a small aerosol can, the device sprays a noxious chemical agent which will *sometimes* blind or temporarily disable an assailant. The most effective spray—mace—is illegal in many areas, and you may find an ordinance against *all* chemical devices where you live. Further, if you ever use one in a street confrontation, be very accurate and *beware!* Unless you squirt the assailant directly in the eyes, he'll probably get very mad and confiscate your little can. Then he'll stomp you into a greasy spot on the sidewalk. And if the wind is blowing in your direction—watch out! The spray might drift back into *your* face—instead of the assailant's—and then you're in real trouble. Still, with a solid hit in the eyes, chemical spray does an admirable job. So don't discount it, but never forget that it has definite limitations. Unbelievable as it may sound, I know a girl who got rattled—somehow she turned the device "bassackwards"—and squirted herself. The mugger almost died laughing!

Do revert to instinct on the streets. You have it, but it's merely gone dormant. A hundred years ago your ancestors survived because their "sixth sense" warned them of marauders, bushwhackers and other unsavory types. To a great degree, it's a matter of mental attitude. First, you must accept the fact that the environment of today is no less hostile than it was in other periods of excessive violence. Then you must condition your reflexes to react without command; attune yourself to the sounds and smells and natural rhythms of the world about you. Finally, with all your senses sharpened, you will begin to develop a "hunch" or a "gut feeling" for anything out of the ordinary. That's the day you can start to rely on instinct. And it's also the day your chances on the street will improve enormously.

Don't resist an armed assailant if you are *unarmed.* Hand over your purse or wallet and let him depart in peace. Of course, there are variations on the theme. If he has a gun, *freeze*—and hope for the best. If he has a knife and attacks, then you're fighting for your life. Take evasive action—perhaps pull the Jackknife you're carrying—and wait for an opening to counterattack. If he's unarmed—merely threatens and demands your money—then you have a choice. Attack or comply. But don't hesitate. Do one or the other instantly, based on a "gut" evaluation of your chances. However, if he's unarmed and attacks, then you have *no* options. React with the correct evasive tactics, then counterattack and *go for the jugular!* He asked for it, so anything goes. Put him down and out, and make sure he stays there.

Don't rely on makeshift weapons. A rat-tail comb or an umbrella or a hatpin *will not* save your life. These "weapons" merely provoke an assailant to greater violence rather than disable him. In a last ditch struggle—particularly if he's armed with a knife—perhaps makeshift weapons will momentarily keep him at a distance. But your hands and feet are vastly more destructive as weapons. Ward him off; take evasive action; use *anything* to thwart his attack. Then pick your spot and move into counterattack. Strike to those vital target areas: throat, nose, kneecap, and stomach/groin. Forget your umbrella, and cripple him with blows that will end the fight. Permanently!

Don't forget your teeth. A fierce bite in the right spot—especially the throat—will scare the daylights out of your assailant. Or if you really sink your teeth and bite down hard, it could finish him off in a matter of seconds. Perhaps the whole idea revolts you. Suddenly you have visions of spurting blood and a mouthful of mangled flesh. Think again! First, the urge to bite comes naturally. It's an instinct you were born with; an instinct that was subverted in childhood. Second, an uninhibited bite, however primeval it sounds, might very well prevent your being raped or murdered. So you have a choice. Shrink from the idea in disgust, and convince yourself it's simply too repugnant an act for any civilized human being. Or use your teeth on an assailant and save your life. Survival is just that elemental, and on the streets you don't get a second chance. Weigh the alternative carefully. It's your life and your teeth—and your decision.

Don't let your guard down. Never assume anything on the streets, least of all the brotherhood and good will of a stranger. One careless moment is all it takes. Then you become that statistic. *Victim mugged and assaulted. Victim raped and forced to perform unnatural acts. Victim DOA.* Yet every victim—even those dead on arrival—have, in a very real sense, victimized themselves. By thoughtless actions and misguided trust and simple naivete about the world around them. So stay alert and key yourself to instant reaction. If you're ambushed on the street, attack or counterattack as the situation dictates. But do it with all the ferocity and speed you can muster. The life you save *will* be your own.

A street attack is a terrifying experience. You may have all the right instincts; execute all the right blows, and still fail. Perhaps your assailant is a blooded veteran, wise to all the tricks. Or perhaps you evade his initial assault and still falter on counterattack. Which means you're in a hairy situation and very much on the defensive. So where do you go from there? What happens next?

Unfortunately, it's quite simple. You either submit or you keep fighting. If you opt for the latter choice, then you must immediately switch tactics. You take evasive action—adopt a defensive posture—and wait for him to blunder. Or perhaps you'll lure him into a mistake and create the opportunity for another counterattack. However it's done, the point remains the same. *You're now on the defensive*! To win, you must await an opening and, in the process, absorb the least amount of punishment possible.

In large measure, your defense will consist of *anticipating* all the blows and kicks previously described. After that, it's a matter of avoiding and/or deflecting everything thrown your way. Do duck and weave, slide away from blows, block them with your arms. All the defensive moves associated with boxing are adaptable to street fighting. You can ward off most of your assailant's punches by constantly shifting position. Also, never be too proud to retreat. Back-pedal, or leap clear, and force him to come at you again. Start fresh, and perhaps you'll create the chance to attack. On counterattack, of course, the short man should slip inside the reach of a taller assailant. Conversely, the tall man gains an edge by delivering kicks and blows from long range.

Defense against kicks is an altogether different matter. If you're unable to avoid the kick, then twist sideways and absorb the impact on your hip/thigh/buttocks. It's essential that you take any kick in a nonvital area, which most especially precludes the kneecap, groin or stomach. Naturally, the best defense is simply to jump back far enough to evade the kick entirely. But if you're aggressive—and you intend to win the fight—then that backward jump is merely a preliminary move. The mongoose kills the cobra by provoking it to strike, then counterattacks while the snake is extended and helpless. The tactic works equally well in a streetfight.

Upon eluding the kick, simultaneously grab your assailant's foot or ankle. Heave up and back with all your strength and dump him on his butt. Without hesitation, swift as the mongoose, step forward and kick him in the jaw as he hits the ground. If that doesn't end it, then shift sideways (avoiding his arms) and kick him at the base of the skull as he attempts to rise. Curiously enough, few men expect to have their leg grabbed in this fashion. So the tactic works if you've got the nerve to pick your spot and move decisively.

It's often impossible to avoid being kicked during those moments you're on the defensive. But if you manage to elude kicks to vital body areas, then you still have a fighting chance. On the streets, that bit of savvy represents the best odds you're likely to obtain.

Hand-to-hand combat is a brutal, sometimes savage business. The individual forced into a streetfight must discard compassion and mercy for the practical realities of survival. A gunfight, and to some degree a knife fight, has about it a sense of the impersonal. It is the weapon itself which inflicts the wound, and with that neat rationalization, a man emotionally disassociates himself from the event. Yet an individual can be maimed or killed in a streetfight with no less certainty. An unprovoked street attack is in itself an animalistic act; by the very nature of the assault, it stands apart from the realm of decency. The mugger/rapist prowls the streets in the way of all predators. His attack is swift and bestial—often cowardly—and always with pitiless disregard for his victim. So what he gets is little more than he deserves and, in all probability, long past due.

The five inflexible rules for survival in hand-to-hand combat:

1. Forget sportsmanship. In streetfights, the law of survival overshadows humanism and fair play.

2. Utilize the element of surprise. Strike first with a blow or kick of an unexpected nature.

3. Never wait for an assailant to start the fight. When threatened, you have both the right and the obligation to defend yourself. So strike first and make it a blow that counts.

4. Strike to vital target areas which instantly neutralize your assailant. The larynx, nose and soft underbelly are key fight-stoppers.

5. Discard inhibitions about dirty fighting. Kick whenever an opportunity presents itself. Once you get an assailant down, keep him down. *By whatever means necessary.*

4

GUNFIGHTING

I never shot at a man in my life
and missed him. I always managed
to beat the other fellow to it by
the sixteenth part of a second.
—Bill Tilghman, U.S. Marshal

Armed Defense is the Free Man's Ultimate Guarantee

WHILE gunpowder was discovered in ancient China, the first recorded use of a handgun occurred in England in 1326 A.D. This particular weapon used a form of gunpowder to fire an arrow. It was representative of a period lasting hundreds of years in which firearms were cumbersome, extremely unreliable and possessed the distinct limitation of firing only one shot. As late as the 16th Century, fully two hundred years after the invention of handguns, the pistol used by cavalrymen misfired so frequently that it was equipped with a bludgeon on one end.

Early in the 19th Century, however, firing mechanisms had been perfected to the point that reasonably sized handguns were being produced. But even then, such weapons remained for the most part single shot devices. Not until 1831, with Samuel Colt's invention of a reliable revolver, were handguns elevated to a position of importance in man's search for practical self-defense. From that point on, the art of gunfighting became a safeguard in the American concept of individual liberty. Thus, while guns have been in use for almost seven centuries, gunfighting as we know it has existed for only slightly over a hundred years.

Unlike close-quarters combat, which had a background of development over thousands of years, gunfighting was a uniquely different form of self-defense. In the mid-1850's there were no time-tested guidelines to follow; then during the half century of the great western expansion, a basic primer evolved on this relatively new, but highly lethal skill. It was a time of trial and error in determining the soundest approach to man's ultimate competition; those who committed the fewest errors lived to tell the tale.

The general principles of gunfighting evolved on the western frontier have changed little in the hundred years since. Though refinements have been added, the basic approach remains the same. And as our ancestors were quick to discover, gunfighting is one of the most unnerving forms of personal combat ever devised by man.

In knife fighting or close combat, the individual is physically involved and must react instinctively to the flow of the action. There is little time for thought or calculation. In gunfighting, however, the element which overshadows all else—including accuracy with a gun—is the cool, unhurried deliberation which ensures that the first shot a man fires is the last shot of the fight.

The brief, violent history of gunfighting abounds with illustrations of individuals who were killed quickly and easily by men who had never fired at a bull's-eye in their lives. Quite often the highly accurate target shooters would empty their pistols in a blinding roar of gunfire, inexplicably missing with every shot, only to be cut down with the first slug fired by their opponent. Frequently the target shooters would even wound their adversaries, as many as two or three times. But since none of the hits were of a killing nature, they still ended up in the dust. What they failed to consider was the question of *speed versus deliberation.*

The single element that separates gunfighter from leadslinger is the nerveless detachment to utilize a *deliberate fraction of a second.* An imperceptible moment of delay which ensures that the first shot fired will accurately strike a vital organ in the body of one's opponent.

The term "deliberate" shouldn't be misconstrued as meaning a leisurely, calculated sighting on an antagonist. Deliberation in a gunfight is represented by the .10 hundredths of a second it takes to guarantee that the gun is aligned on the vital chest-stomach area of one's antagonist. For anyone who has spent time firing a pistol in rapid fire situations, this hairline distinction is very real and quite clear. Through hours of practice and the expenditure of hundreds of rounds, they have found that this fragmentary hesitation generally means the difference between a miss or a solid kill shot.

The vast majority of people are unaware that a pistol is essentially an inaccurate weapon—particularly in a stress situation where the shot must be fired in a half-second or less. Short-barreled, difficult to stablize in the firing position, the pistol leaves much to be desired in terms of accuracy. The longer barrel of a shoulder weapon in itself does much to ensure well-placed shots. The handgun, by its very nature, means less control and greater probability of a miss—unless you impose rigid self-discipline in order to avoid the trap of hurrying the shot.

And the only shot that counts is the one that hits a vital organ. Once you realize that deliberation in a gunfight is the stark difference between life and death, then the correlation of cool detachment and steady shooting takes on increased meaning.

Another psychological pitfall which must be overcome in a gunfight is the almost obsessive compulsion to run or dodge. In other words, the temptation to present a moving target to your assailant. Numerous gun battles between police and criminals have pitted a dodging adversary against an opponent who stood perfectly still and fired with unflustered deliberation. Virtually without exception, the moving target ended up dead while his opponent calmly reloaded and waited for the undertaker to arrive.

Firing a pistol with accuracy while on the run is one of the most difficult feats known to man. Conversely, hitting a moving man-sized target is comparatively simple, particularly if the individual firing has taken a solid stance and knows something about leading a moving object.

During World War II a British Commando training officer devised a system for training men to fire a pistol while running, dodging and performing gyrations more commonly associated with halfbacks on a football field. Only later did it become apparent that the percentage of men who could perform this feat in combat was practically nil. Unfortunately, many of the training officer's students died trying to accomplish a trick that even deadeye exhibition shooters would never attempt. The conclusion is rather obvious.

Another hazard that must be avoided is the temptation to run a bluff, fire a warning shot, or shoot to wound. The record indicates that where men attempted to bluff in a gunfight, almost without exception they ended up the guests of honor at their own wake. Less frequent, but still not without incidence, were those foolhardy souls who fired a warning shot or tried to wound their opponent out of some misguided sense of humanity. While noble to the extreme, their effort generally got the wrong man killed. Unlike many forms of competition between men, gunfighting is serious business. When the shooting ceases, there's only one score that counts: who's alive and who isn't. Whenever another man has shown by hostile action that he intends gunplay, the wisest course is to shoot first—and make certain that the first slug fired is the last.

Only in storybook nobility do heroes attempt to run a bluff, or humanely wound their antagonists. In real life such men rapidly become compassionate stiffs.

Once the shooting starts there is a merciless quality necessary to survival in a gunfight. Psychologically, this is one of the most difficult hurdles for the thou-shalt-not-kill humanist to overcome. History records the untimely burial of many men who fired first, hit their opponent, and then stopped shooting. Though it was obvious that their adversaries were far from disabled, much less mortally wounded, they simply couldn't bring themselves to finish the job. What made them hesitate, when they could easily have ended the fight with a second shot, will never be known. Their reason was buried with them.

The strength and resiliency of the human body is awe inspiring. There are many instances of wounded men only moments away from death who somehow found the mortal tenacity to draw, fire and kill their antagonist. Survival dictates that once a man has pulled the trigger he must continue firing until his opponent is either dead or so completely disabled that he no longer poses a threat. Only under the most extraordinary circumstances, such as a direct hit in the heart or head, should fewer than two or three shots be fired. Two direct hits in the chest-stomach area will generally stop any man. But merciless as it may sound, if he is still attempting to bring his gun into play, then he must be fired on until the threat no longer exists. A New York City detective once proved the point the hard way, establishing some sort of record for the involuntary collection of lead. Taken unaware, he survived a gunfight in which he was shot six times, twice in the chest, once in each shoulder and once in each arm.

There are instances, of course, where an individual may be faced with two or more assailants. The great temptation in such a situation is to fire one shot at each adversary in turn, hoping that every slug will have a lethal effect. In addition to the possibility of missed shots, there is the greater probability that even a direct hit will not instantaneously disable an opponent. Outnumbered though he may be, the individual involved in such a gunfight must somehow dredge up the nerve to fire twice at each antagonist, taking them one at a time without thought of the incoming slugs fired by those not yet engaged. The chances of one surviving a gunfight with two or three opponents are slim at best. But if he fires only one shot at each antagonist the likelihood of his reaching old age is virtually nonexistent.

Briefly, it may be stated that the mental composure so vital to deliberation and unhurried shooting transcends in importance any other factor in gunfighting. It is all very well to be the fastest draw in town, or the most accurate target shot in the county, but these attributes are of small consequence if the man involved fails to utilize that split-hair of a second necessary to ensure a kill shot. Everyone is familiar with fighters who are unbeatable in the gym, or quarterbacks who are brilliant on the practice field, only to miss punches in the ring and hurriedly dump passes when faced with charging linemen in a

The Ultimate Tranquilizer! Stubby scattergun loaded with 12-gauge buckshot. A sure-fire cure for what ails an armed intruder.

game. The same principle holds true for men who lack the detachment to face the gun of an antagonist without becoming flustered. The essential and rather permanent difference being that the man who comes unglued in a gunfight generally ends up on a slab in the morgue.

Normally, when men think of gunfights their minds conjure up an image of two opponents blazing away at one another with pistols. Undoubtedly, the romantic heritage of cowboys, frontier marshals and the Colt six-shooter has done much to establish the pistol as the primary weapon of self-defense. Rarely disclosed is the fact that a large percentage of the men killed in the Old West were downed by the most formidable weapon on the frontier, the double-barrel shotgun. The essential reason that more marshals lived to reach old age than did outlaws was that the lawmen were frequently armed with a sawed-off scattergun. Though to a lesser degree, the same thought holds true for modern law enforcement officers, who rely chiefly on the 12-gauge pump shotgun, commonly referred to as a riot gun.

Somehow the shotgun has never achieved the romantic aura of the revolver. Perhaps, in Americans' inherent drive for fairness, such a weapon seems a bit unsportsmanlike. For men involved in gunfights, however, the matter of sportsmanship runs a poor second to survival. With few exceptions, the men using shotguns generally walk away from a shootout unscathed.

For sheer killing power, and indisputable accuracy, the shotgun is unmatched by any weapon ever used in the history of gunfighting. When loaded with 00 buckshot, which contains nine lead balls (each approximately the diameter of a .32 caliber slug) the impact on a man receiving such a charge is stunning, to say the least. If he isn't killed outright, the shock to his central nervous system is so damaging that for all practical purposes he is permanently out of the fight. At a range of seven to ten yards, which is the distance involved in the majority of gunfights, the nine slugs in 00 buckshot inflict an entrance wound that can be covered by a man's outstretched hand.

The damage those nine slugs do internally to anyone, and the size of the exit hole at short ranges, is sufficiently obvious that no gory recounting is necessary. Understandably, any man hit by a charge of 00 buckshot in the chest-stomach area is generally only a few moments away from death—either from massive shock, internal hemorrhaging or obliteration of a vital organ.

In terms of accuracy, particularly at short ranges, the man firing such a weapon is virtually assured of neutralizing his assailant. When involved in a gunfight at night, there is no weapon in existence that provides a man with a better chance of survival. Though he may be firing only at a shadow or movement in a darkened situation, the likelihood of a kill-shot is extremely great. Even a leg wound or an arm wound is still of sufficient impact to discourage an opponent from carrying the fight further.

Many a gunfight has been forestalled completely by the simple act of one man aiming a shotgun in the general direction of his opponent's midriff. For raw psychological intimidation there has never been a weapon to match the shotgun. To say that the effect on a man staring into the cavernous bore of a 12-gauge scattergun is mentally debilitating would be an understatement of the first magnitude. Only a fool, or an extremely desperate man, would make a move toward his weapon when someone has the drop on him with a shotgun. Those who have tried such a feat more often than not experienced a quick and painless demise.

The homeowner who has neither the time nor the inclination to practice diligently with a pistol would be well advised to buy himself a shotgun. There is generally no restriction on the purchase of shotguns, regardless of where one resides. Morever, it is legally permissible to cut the barrel down to something approximating sawed-off length, which for ease of handling and stunning power at short ranges provides an incomparable weapon. While Federal law prohibits fashioning a truly sawed-off type weapon, the barrel of a shotgun can legally be reduced to 18″. Measuring from buttplate to the tip of the barrel, the minimum overall length allowed is 26″. As a practical matter, a weapon this size compares equally to the sawed-off shotguns once used by frontier lawmen. Whether double-barrel or pump, the shotgun is undeniably the finest means of self-defense available to the general public.

The point is worth stressing. *Stubby scatterguns are both the most practical and the most effective weapon for home defense.* There are several reasons why you should forget the pistol and consider a shotgun instead:

1. A shotgun is simple to operate and any adult (or teen-ager) can learn to handle it properly with minimum instruction. I once taught a friend's wife (who was literally petrified by guns) to place every load in the chest-stomach area of a silhouette target. It took less than an hour to overcome her fear and instruct her in the combat technique of firing a scattergun. *NOTE:* When firing live ammo, ear plugs or acoustical muffs will block out the sound of the shot, which generally affects the beginner much more than recoil.
2. A shotgun requires little marksmanship (even under stress) so it's the perfect weapon for the *average* homeowner. Ammo is the vital factor. The 12-gauge 00 buckshot, with nine .32 caliber pellets, is considered the standard defense load. However, #4 buckshot, which hurls twenty-seven .24 caliber slugs, is equally lethal. In darkened situations, particularly at longer ranges, it also offers greater probability of a solid hit. Personally, I use both loads. In the Remington Model 870 pump, which I keep downstairs, I load 00 and #4 alternately. In the custom-made double-barrel (18-1/4″ barrels), which I keep in the upstairs bedroom, I load the first tube with 00 and the second tube with #4. The combination is calculated to handle any situation I might encounter. Whichever load you choose, there is small likelihood of return fire. One shotgun blast will neutralize an intruder *instantly.* The reason is the massive wound that occurs (pathologists call it a

rathole wound) when the charge strikes at close range.

3. A shotgun is particularly well suited to women. Although the recoil of a 12-gauge is perhaps a bit harsh on the ladies, a 20-gauge is perfect. The recoil is quite moderate, and loaded with #3 buckshot (twenty .25 caliber slugs) it delivers a devastating punch. The double-barrel scattergun is perhaps preferable for women, especially if there are small (curious) children in the house. It is quick to load, even in the dark, and requires no manual operation; merely click off the safety and pull the trigger. The result is not only persuasive, but highly conclusive; for a woman alone at night, it provides the optimum in moral support. An excellent choice is the Savage Fox Model B: double-barrel, twin triggers and 20-gauge. *NOTE:* To eliminate confusion, perhaps we had best define *gauge* and *caliber.* Gauge is the interior diameter of a shotgun barrel. Caliber is the outside diameter of a bullet or round slug, expressed in fractions of an inch. Thus, a 20-gauge #3 buckshot shell can be packed with twenty .25 caliber slugs.

4. Indoors, where maneuverability is a factor, the stubby scattergun is unsurpassed. Remington and Ithaca market pump shotguns with 20″ barrels, and the Winchester pump has a 22″ barrel. Although American double-barrel shotguns have standard long tubes, I personally consider it worth the extra cost (for home defense) to have a gunsmith take a hacksaw to the barrels. The double-barrel 12-gauge I had custom built also has only one trigger; with a quick double twitch of the trigger finger, I can actually get off two shots faster than with an automatic. If expense is a fac-

tor, then order a Rossi Overland from your gun dealer. Patterned on the old Wells Fargo mini-cannon, this imported version is double-barrel (exposed hammers) with 20″ barrels. The key point, of course, is to combine ease of handling with maximum firepower. By any equation, that calls for a shotgun with stubbed-off barrels. *NOTE:* In gunfighting there's no such thing as overkill. Use all the firepower you are capable of handling, whether it is 12-gauge Magnum buckshot or a .44 Magnum pistol. Your first shot must count, so experiment with a number of weapons and determine the maximum firepower you can control with accuracy.

5. A shotgun may be purchased without a permit, although some cities require that the weapon be registered. Where handguns are prohibited by law, this becomes a decisive factor. Kill an intruder with an illegal pistol and you could end up behind bars; blow him away with a shotgun (on your home turf, of course) and the law is on your side. Moreover, there are literally dozens of different shotgun models from which you can select. Both automatic and over/under models are generally too expensive for home defense. But there is a wide range of single-shot, double-barrel and pump scatterguns which can be purchased for well under $200. If you feel $200 is an exorbitant price to pay for home defense, then simply pick up the evening paper and glance through the headlines. Approximately sixty people are murdered every day, with the regularity of clockwork—over 20,000 homicides a year. A shotgun could be the cheapest life insurance you ever bought. And it's a lot less expensive than a fancy funeral.

Understandably, there are many situations which will preclude the use of a shoulder weapon. In such moments the individual concerned with his own self-defense must be prepared to use a pistol. The first, and certainly one of the most crucial steps in that preparation is the selection of a weapon.

For the most part, the choice between a revolver or an automatic is strictly a matter of individual preference. Virtually all law enforcement agencies require their officers to use revolvers, based on the theory that automatics offer a greater risk of jammed cartridges. Thus a lawman could conceivably find himself in a gunfight with a weapon that suddenly becomes inoperable. Unless an automatic is cleaned regularly, such a possibility certainly exists. Still, given the exactitude of modern gunmaking, the probability of a jammed cartridge or a spent cartridge failing to eject is rather slight.

Some men feel that an automatic provides great advantage in that the hammer remains cocked after each shot, thus requiring far less trigger pull. This is undeniably a factor in accuracy during rapid fire. Many individuals, on the other hand, believe that a revolver is more reliable, better balanced and easier to use in quick-draw situations.

In the final analysis, the selection of a pistol is a deeply individualistic thing, and the choice is generally decided on some emotional factor rather than one of practicality. As long as the gun has some semblance of balance, there is little difference in accuracy at short ranges, whether a man is firing a Colt Peacemaker or the most modern double-action automatic. Where the quick draw is concerned, speed is dependent on the man, not the weapon. An automatic can be brought into action as rapidly as a revolver by any man who cares to practice that particular skill.

As we shall see, however, the quick draw is possibly

the least important of those skills necessary to survival in a gunfight. Clearly, the selection of a pistol should never be based on that factor alone.

The major considerations in choosing a weapon are grip, caliber, balance and purpose. Whether a man's hand is large or small plays an important role in how securely a particular pistol will seat in his grip. This is especially true for women. For accuracy in rapid-fire situations, where the gun is bucking and jumping with each shot, the weapon must seat firmly and naturally in a normal grip. Crimping or straining of the hand to meet the conformation of the pistol will drastically reduce accuracy. An individual selecting a pistol would do well to take his time, handle a number of weapons, and choose the one which seems to be a comfortable extension of his own hand.

The caliber of any weapon selected for self-defense must be predicated on the fact that its primary function is to neutralize an assailant with the minimum number of shots. This being the case, it would be courting disaster to choose any pistol of less than .380 caliber. Smaller calibers such as .25 or .32 will decidedly kill, but there is a distinct possibility that a man mortally wounded by such slugs will still be able to get off a killing shot. On the other hand, a man vitally wounded by a .357 Magnum, 9mm or .38 Special will be far less likely to retain the control necessary for accurate shooting. Though the .45 ACP and the .44 Magnum have much greater killing power, they are generally somewhat less accurate in the hands of any but the skilled gunman. For that reason they should be avoided by the *average* homeowner seeking a reliable means of self-defense.

There is a wide choice of weapons available for men. Both Colt and Smith & Wesson make a variety of revolvers in the medium calibers, and the 9mm double-action automatic marketed by Smith & Wesson is one of the finest defensive weapons ever manufactured. Women generally have greater difficulty in controlling even the medium calibers, and thus their selection is somewhat more restricted. Nonetheless, there are a number of small-framed and equally small-handled pistols available in a range of calibers (the .380 auto is particularly well suited to women).

Like the proper grip, the balance of a pistol is an extremely personal thing—a matter of feel—and to a large extent a matter of opinion. Generally speaking, a large, heavy gun will feel balanced to big men with large hands, yet extremely cumbersome to men of smaller stature. Conversely, the shorter, lighter weapon will seem to find its own level in the hand of an average-sized individual. But a bigger man may find it almost impossible to orient the same pistol with the target. Balance in a gun is something that one feels or senses. It can't be measured or weighed or observed visually, for in reality it is an intangible rationalization between individual and weapon. When a man hefts a pistol, it either balances perfectly or else lies in his hand like an unmanageable clod. There never seems to be any middle ground, and if the gun doesn't balance the first time he hefts it, then it probably never will. To a great degree, the balance is determined by the relationship between the grip of the hand and the length of the barrel, and perhaps this is why men prefer guns that correspond to their own size. Still, any statement concerning balance is almost a generalization.

The relationship between a man and his gun is an extremely personal phenomenon, and only by hefting a number of pistols will he find the one that magically aligns itself each time he lays it on the target. But find it he must. For in the fractionalized seconds of a gunfight, he must have utter confidence that the gun in hand is perfectly balanced and always aligned on his opponent.

The purpose for which a pistol is intended will also

have great bearing on the type of gun a man selects. Self-defense being the primary consideration, he should choose a weapon for use at relatively short ranges, with a barrel of medium length to provide greater accuracy, and of sufficient killing power to ensure that his opponent will be downed when hit. Long-barreled guns of the .45 caliber or .44 Magnum class, as well as the small snub-nosed variety, should be left to professionals who have the time to acquire the particular skills that such weapons demand. Adequate self-defense requires a gun which is easily controlled and relatively quick to put into action—one with which the average citizen can practice on weekends and still be assured of stopping an antagonist should he ever be attacked.

Television shows and movies would have the public believe that a person needs only to point a pistol in the general direction of an adversary and the bullet will magically find its mark. In the world of make-believe we often see people who have never before handled a gun suddenly pick up a revolver and down their antagonist with a plumb-center shot straight through the heart. Not long ago, on one of the more popular television westerns, the protagonist jerked both guns simultaneously, and with flame spouting from each hip shattered six whiskey glasses that had been thrown into the air. Frequently, the hero will draw his six-gun with blinding speed and humanely place a slug through his opponent's shoulder. Or even more ludicrous, shoot the gun out of the other man's hand! Such superhuman accuracy is commonplace on celluloid, and for sheer fabricated nonsense these scenes are unrivaled by even the Mother Goose fairy tales.

One can only speculate as to how many everyday citizens would lose their lives the instant they tried to duplicate such feats when involved in a real gunfight. With constant daily practice, often firing hundreds of rounds in a week's time, there are a few highly gifted men who can achieve spectacular accuracy with instinctive pointing of the weapon. Ed McGivern, who in 1934 placed five shots in an Ace of Spades in 2/5ths of a second, was one such individual. But since the advent of gunfighting, the number of men who could accomplish such accuracy would comprise no more than a meager handful. It is extremely doubtful that there is a law enforcement officer in America today who would even attempt such a performance. The reason is a rather sound one: men who are familiar with weapons recognize the inherent limitations within the unpredictable mix of man, gun and speed.

Few men will react in the heat of a gunfight as they do when shooting at targets. The focus of concentration, therefore, must be on the largest possible lethal area—the chest-stomach bulk of an assailant. Though a man with a slug in his bowels is rarely killed outright, the likelihood of deliberately placing a shot in the heart or head during a gunfight is extremely remote. Some years back a famous peace officer commented:

> I hope you never have to shoot any man, but if you do, shoot him in the guts near the navel. You may not make a fatal shot, but he will get a shock that will paralyze his brain and arm so much that the fight is all over.

The homeowner or citizen who wishes to master the pistol as a means of self-defense would be wise to follow this perceptive commandment. Moreover, since the handgun will be used primarily as a combat weapon, it is just as well to practice on man-sized silhouette targets from the very outset. *NOTE:* Silhouette targets are inexpensive and can be bought from your local gun dealer.

Unless you already have some experience with your weapon it would be advisable to expend at least one hundred rounds on slow-fire practice in the beginning. Of

Figure 1.

equal importance, you would be wise *always* to use the double-hand combat grip. Hold the gun in both hands as illustrated in *Fig. 1*; support the gun hand from beneath with the free hand. By *pushing forward* with the gun hand and *pulling back* with the supporting hand, it is possible to lock the gun on target in a viselike grip. The push-pull double-hand grip provides maximum resistance to recoil, and ensures instant realignment on the target after firing. This method is particularly good for women, and will provide an invaluable aid in achieving consistent accuracy.

The proper grip of the gun hand is with the center line of the pistol frame bisecting the "notch" formed by the thumb and forefinger. The thumb should squeeze naturally around the handle, folding across the top of the middle finger. The trigger finger should remain free—it must *never* support the pistol—and should wrap around the trigger in a natural curl. Proper trigger control simply consists of squeezing *straight through* the trigger. A smooth, steady motion without jerks or interruption. The supporting hand, meanwhile, wraps around the front of the gun hand, clutching tightly, and pulls backward with constant pressure.

So now you're ready to fire. Extend both arms, using the combat grip, and swing the gun up to eye level. Aim carefully and squeeze off each shot at a specific target, preferably the dark circle centered on the silhouette. Start at ten yards, then gradually work back to twenty yards and finally thirty yards, carefully observing each shot and the manner in which distance can change perspective. With the expenditure of a hundred rounds, most men will have become accustomed to the jump and buck of their weapon. Equally important, they will have developed an appreciation for the fact that it requires self-discipline and concentration to fire a pistol accurately even when using sights. The next step is to master *instinctive pointing,* that is aiming accurately without using the sights.

Aiming instinctively is somewhat like pointing one's finger, in that the pistol is considered an extension of the arm. Very few men are born with the ability to fire a pistol in this offhand manner with any degree of accuracy. But almost all have the capacity to learn instinctive shooting if they are willing to spend adequate time practicing. Generally, it takes a number of sessions on the target range for an individual of average coordination to develop the sense of instinctive aiming. If he is firing live ammunition, it can become rather expensive. Since there is a more effective method of achieving the same proficiency, it is well worth the expenditure to purchase a pellet pistol.

Figure 2. Combat Stance for range of 7–15 yards. Excellent pellet gun for mastering instinctive aim is the Crosman 38 Combat Revolver. Powered by CO_2 gas, the revolver is accurate and fires pellets on an extremely flat trajectory.

Figure 3. Combat Stance for range of 3–7 yards. Crosman 38 Combat Revolver, which fires .22 caliber pellets, will hasten understanding of instinctive aim.

Like the air rifles one used in childhood, this is a pistol which fires lead pellets and can be obtained in almost any sporting goods store. In most cities these pellet pistols can be purchased without a permit; it is generally legal to fire them anywhere on one's own property. The significant point in utilizing a pellet pistol to master instinctive aiming is the fact that *the pellet can be observed visually* while it is in flight. Obviously then, while watching the pellet in flight, this clarifies the relationship between pointed gun and the trajectory of the slug.

Initially it is advisable to set up a silhouette target in the backyard or garage. Pace off five yards and extend both arms fully, using the combat grip. Look at your target directly over the top of the pellet pistol and fire without using the sights *(Fig. 2).* Within a short time it will become apparent (while watching the pellet's path to the target) just where the pistol must be pointed in order to place the shot accurately. After some degree of skill is attained, it is then recommended that the pistol be held down beside the leg, raised quickly to the extended arm position and fired. Generally it will take some time, and possibly another box of pellets, before the coordination of arm movement, instinctive aiming and rapid fire is effected. Once you achieve consistent accuracy in this manner, then repeat the entire procedure, and when the pistol comes on target fire *two shots.* Over a period of time, by careful observation of the arm in relation to the flight of the pellet, you will develop a sixth sense for aiming the pistol. Thereafter, you can then accurately place three or four shots in the target in rapid succession.

The next step is to hold the pistol at your side, raise it quickly to a position halfway between waist and shoulder level, and fire *(Fig. 3).* Keep in mind, as you raise the pistol with your gun hand, the supporting hand is simultaneously raised, arriving in position to grip the gun hand an instant before the shot is fired.

Once again, this new position will require time to affect coordination and aim. During all phases of firing, some specific target should be the point of aim. This provides a basis of comparison between the pointed gun and the strike of the pellet. In rapid fire most people have a tendency to shoot high, usually caused by jerking the trigger. As a result, it is wise in the beginning to hold on the stomach area. When accuracy has been achieved with regularity from the position in *Fig. 3,* then the distance should be increased to seven yards and the procedures outlined above for *Figs. 2 and 3* repeated in their entirety. When accuracy is attained at seven yards, then the range should be increased to ten yards and the same procedures repeated once again.

Generally there will be a great temptation to fire the pellet pistol from the hip, in imitation of the movie cowboys and gunfighters. Although entertaining, it is an extremely bad habit to develop. Hip-shooting at a target won't do anything more damaging than waste a good deal of ammunition. But in a gunfight it is the prime qualification for a quick burial. That fact alone makes it a practice worth avoiding.

Which brings us to a cardinal rule that is *never* to be violated: Only in an extreme emergency, when your opponent is literally at point blank range (three yards or less) should you fire a pistol with *one hand.* The technique is illustrated in *Fig. 4.* The arm is extended at belt level, elbow cocked and forward of the hip, forearm parallel to the ground. In a sense, you *throw* the gun at your opponent, halting it quickly on the upswing and locking it into position. Then you pull the trigger at the *exact instant* the upward momentum is halted. *And you keep on pulling the trigger until your opponent is out of action.* At point blank range, you cannot afford to take chances, so you dose him with a spray of lead that will get the job done. But remember, this method is to be used only in a

Figure 4. Combat Stance for point blank range. Crosman 38 Combat Revolver is double action, and an excellent pellet gun for rapid fire face-to-face training.

face-to-face emergency! Any attempt by the *average homeowner* to use it at greater distances will likely get the wrong man killed.

Eventually, you will reach a point where your instinctive aim with the pellet pistol brings about well-placed shots on a consistent basis. The fact that you might be unable to group shots in a relatively small area, such as the heart, is unimportant. The critical factor is whether you can score repeatedly in the vital chest-stomach area, firing single and double shots from the positions in *Figs. 2 and 3* at short ranges. These two positions provide the basic stance for accurate, instinctive rapid fire, while the range of 5–10 yards is that involved in the majority of gunfights. Thus, until consistent results are obtained with the pellet pistol, there is nothing to be gained in progressing further. Once instinctive aim has been mastered, however, you can then advance to firing live ammunition.

It is worth noting that many women have an innate fear of firearms, which usually has a drastic effect on their ability to hit the target. Normally the woman who desires to learn the use of a pistol as a means of self-defense begins practicing immediately with live ammunition. The noise, muzzle blast and recoil quite often are too much, too quickly—making her a worse shot than if she had never had any lessons at all. Utilizing the pellet pistol as discussed above, before progressing to live ammunition, will give the woman a sense of confidence, while at the same time lessening her fear of firearms.

Should the homeowner's preference lean toward a shotgun as means of self-defense (which I strongly recommend), then the procedure is much the same as that involved in the use of a pistol. Mastering the shoulder weapon, if anything, is simpler than learning to employ a handgun. As an initial step in gaining a feel for instinctive aiming, you should purchase a BB rifle.

Utilizing the same target, ranges and procedures outlined for the pistol, begin learning how a shoulder weapon reacts when fired from an offhand position *(Fig. 5).* In this position, the left leg is extended forward with the body in a slight crouch. The forepart of the weapon is grasped with the left hand, and the stock is clasped firmly to the side by the right arm and elbow. When the position is properly affected, the left forearm and the weapon will be parallel with the ground. Thus, in whatever direction the left leg moves the body must follow, and the weapon is perfectly aligned at waist level on any target to the front. With only a little practice, you will be able to place shot after shot in the target, rarely experiencing a miss. With a solid stance, and the weapon braced firmly against your side, the recoil will be absorbed by your body; even

Figure 5.

with a 12-gauge shotgun the barrel will seldom waver from the target after firing.

If the situation and time permit, of course, the weapon should *always* be fired from the standard shoulder position. Accuracy increases by *quantum leaps* when the butt of a shotgun is tucked into your shoulder and fired by looking directly over the top of the barrel. But only in the most extreme emergency should it ever be fired from any offhand position other than that shown in *Fig. 5.* Offhand firing of a shoulder weapon when it is improperly braced leads to great inaccuracy; the chances are that in a gunfight you would never have the opportunity of firing a second shot. By constantly utilizing the position shown in *Fig. 5,* however, virtually every shot will be placed directly in the chest-stomach area of the target. The individual who masters this particular technique is a formidable opponent indeed.

It is worth noting that *all* women (even those who own a pistol) should be trained in the use of a shotgun. Whether a woman is married or single, she is often alone at night, and there is no better weapon for defense of the home than a scattergun loaded with buckshot.

When men start working with a pistol, there is a curious temptation to begin practicing the fast draw almost immediately. The unfortunate aspect of moving into fast draw work too quickly is that it can create many bad habits and permanently serve as a deterrent to accuracy. Regardless of how fast a man can draw a pistol, he is bordering on suicide if he hasn't first attained the ability to place each shot with unfailing accuracy.

Once you're ready to progress into firing live ammunition, you should again utilize a silhouette target, alternating the range between five and ten yards. Assuming the positions in *Figs. 2 and 3,* expend at least twenty rounds in each position to ensure that you have the same feel for instinctive aim with a loaded weapon that you had gotten with the pellet pistol. Initially, you should fire only single shots, relaxing and reassuming the position after each round is fired. Close observation of where the slugs strike the target will provide an insight into how the body position or arm level must be changed.

In the beginning, your feet should be spread comfortably, toes on an even line, with the body relaxed. Simultaneously, as the pistol is brought to bear on target, the knees are flexed and the body drops into a slight crouch *(Figs. 2 and 3).* Should you experience a tendency to fire either to the right or to the left, simply move your feet to change the flight of the bullet. Moving the left foot forward will tend to place the slug farther to the right, while moving the right foot forward will throw the bullet to the left. In this manner the horizontal placement of the slug can be controlled. Once you learn the correct placement for your feet, then practice moving into that position until it becomes an automatic reaction any time you extend the pistol.

The vertical flight of the bullet must also be taken into consideration. The level of the gun arm controls the vertical path of the slug, thus whenever your arm is tilted high or low the bullet will strike the target correspondingly. In *Fig. 2,* the gun arm is extended at shoulder level, elbow locked, with the underside of the arm (from wrist to shoulder) parallel to the ground. Should any part of your gun arm fail to be parallel with the ground (wrist flexed either up or down; elbow cocked, etc.) the slug will quite naturally follow the line of aim and strike the target either high or low.

In *Fig. 3,* although the elbow is cocked, the forearm (from wrist to elbow) is parallel to the ground, held approximately halfway between waist and shoulder level. Thus should any part of your forearm be out of level, or the wrist flexed, the bullet will strike somewhere above or below dead center on the target. When properly executed, the position in *Fig. 2* should place a shot directly in the chest area, while the position in *Fig. 3* should score a hit in the stomach area. From either position, when the hit is misplaced it becomes evident that some part of your arm is not level. The high or low strike of the bullet then indicates what type of correction must be made. If any great difficulty is experienced in determining or correcting the problem, it is advisable to stand sideways to a mirror. Rapidly extend the pistol to the firing position, then check your arm or forearm level in the reflection of the mirror. In this manner the mistake becomes readily apparent.

Once some degree of accuracy has been attained firing single shots from the standard positions, you should then advance to something approximating draw and fire. Relax in an upright stance—with the pistol held at your side—then drop into a crouch, extend the weapon to firing position, hesitate momentarily to ensure alignment on the target, and fire. Over a period of time the length of the hesitation necessary to ensure accuracy will lessen. Finally, there comes a fluid movement of your arm, with only a fractionalized pause before the trigger is squeezed.

Before giving any thought to drawing a pistol from a holster, it is highly recommended that you fire a minimum of one hundred rounds as outlined above. Only in this manner will you be able to develop the rapid fire accuracy so vital to survival in a gunfight. When consistent accuracy has been achieved firing single shots, then the same procedure should be followed firing two shots in succession as the gun comes to bear on target.

It should be stressed that the solid stance of the body, in conjunction with the level, extended arm, are the determining factors in insuring accuracy. Thus, whenever firing on a target, it must be faced squarely by the entire body if consistent hits are to be obtained. Attempting to shoot by moving only the arm in the direction of the target generally results in more misses than hits, which would rather quickly take on fatal undertones in a gunfight. Obviously, whether one is firing on a single opponent, or firing alternately on two or more assailants, the body must be moved to face each adversary in the same motion that the gun is brought to bear. Very few men are capable of standing in a fixed position and snap-shooting in different directions with anything approaching accuracy. *Only after years of disciplined practice, and the expenditure of thousands of rounds of ammunition, does this tactic become practical.*

Regarding the two standard firing positions, it should also be noted that the position in *Fig. 2* is highly advisable for any shot over seven yards, whereas the position in *Fig. 3* is more adaptable to close-range fast shooting.

Should the range extend past fifteen yards you will find accuracy greatly increased by using the sights, or else sighting quickly along the top of the barrel. Of course, should the situation permit, bracing your gun hand against a solid object, such as a wall, will vastly improve accuracy, which in the final analysis is the only thing that counts.

When you have at last achieved accuracy firing by instinctive aim—that is, when the missed shot becomes the exception rather than the rule—then and only then should you give any thought to working on the fast draw. As mentioned previously, the fast draw is undoubtedly the least important element involved in a gunfight. Any detailed study of gunfighting indicates that in the vast majority of shootouts the antagonists knew that danger was impending and already had their guns out before the shooting started. Naturally, there have been many instances where two men started with an even break for their guns, but of all recorded gunfights, such affairs represent only a small percentage. Even then, it was the accurate shooter, rather than the fastest gun, who remained standing when the smoke had cleared.

So it all comes down to a matter of *accuracy versus speed.* In an overwhelming number of gunfights the man who got off the first shot ended up in a funeral parlor, while his slower but more deliberate opponent lived to fight another day. Clearly, the fast draw has limitations where gunfights are concerned—sometimes fatal limitations. It should be approached with a realistic perspective as to its overall value in the matter of survival. Captain Bill Jordan, who served nearly three decades with the U. S. Border Patrol, made the point with indisputable logic when he stated: "Speed's fine but accuracy's final."

With that thought in mind, you should approach the fast draw as nothing more than a means of placing the gun in the firing position—in the shortest possible time.

From that point on it remains a matter of deliberate, instinctive aim to ensure that the first shot fired will strike the vital chest-stomach area. *The hand can place the gun in a firing position faster than instinct can accurately aim it.* For this reason alone there must always be that fragmentary moment which is utilized to assure a direct hit. *It should take as much time to squeeze the trigger as it did to draw the gun.* Whenever there is a disparity between the two, the result is rather predictably a missed shot. When involved in a gunfight, the man who values his life will allow just as much time for firing the shot as he did for jerking the gun. Otherwise it might well be his first and only gunfight.

Before you give any thought to the fast draw, it must first be decided exactly how the pistol is to be carried. For the individual concerned with self-defense this can be a critical decision. Except in extraordinary circumstances, the homeowner would already have gun in hand when danger threatens. But for the man who is actually going to carry a pistol on his person, the choice between hip holster, shoulder holster or cross-draw holster can be a vital factor. Generally speaking, the hip holster attached to the belt just above the right trouser pocket provides the quickest access and fastest draw for a man with or without a coat. Both the shoulder holster and the cross-draw holster (carried on the left side) are slightly slower in that the hand must move to the opposite side of the body before the draw is begun. Obviously this adds to the total elapsed time necessary to bring the gun into a firing position.

Yet selection of a holster, like choice of a weapon, is determined to a great extent by personal preference. In the final analysis, the time differential in drawing from various types of holsters probably has little bearing on the end result of a gunfight. Whether spring loaded or steel lined, it seems doubtful that the rig itself would

Figure 6. Smith & Wesson Model 39 holstered in Safariland Model 6 with safety strap.

ever be that meaningful when the chips are down. Whichever holster the individual feels most comfortable with is the one that will be fastest for him. For it is from this holster that the gun will come most naturally to his touch and seem to spring unaided into his hand. *NOTE:* Unless licensed to carry a gun, it is illegal to have a concealed weapon on one's person. This law is applicable throughout the United States. It also applies to carrying a loaded gun *anywhere* in an automobile. If you decide to carry a pistol for self-defense—regardless of the law—then keep in mind you run the risk of being fined and/or imprisoned.

The hip holster shown in *Fig. 6* is not only the type most commonly used, but it is also the one most frequently associated with the fast draw. Though most men use the same type of holster, there are still two schools of

Figure 7.

Figure 8.

Figure 9.

thought concerning technique. One faction believes that the gun should be pushed backward out of the holster with the butt of the hand, then shoved forward into the firing position. This method is advocated by those who prefer to cock the hammer as the pistol is being drawn. The backward motion of the hand gains control of the weapon while the thumb simultaneously cocks the hammer. For the average individual, however, these movements seem a bit unnatural and require months of intense practice before any degree of proficiency can be attained.

The second method is to bring the arm in a forward sweeping movement from the side, grasping and drawing the gun in one sustained motion *(Figs. 7, 8 and 9).* In this draw, the hand grasps the pistol butt, jerking it up and forward in the same movement, and only after the gun clears the holster is the index finger inserted into the trigger guard. If desirable, the hammer can be cocked as the pistol comes out of the holster. However, this greatly increases the chances of a shot being fired accidentally. It should *never* be attempted until you have become well versed in drawing and firing, utilizing the double-action trigger pull.

In the forward-motion draw, the barrel trails slightly behind the hand as it clears leather. Then it is whipped up and forward until the arm locks the gun in the firing position. The essential element in this or any other type of fast draw is in gaining initial control of the weapon. The gun must be taken hold of with firmness and authority: the pistol butt planted solidly against the heel of the palm; the thumb and fingers gripped exactly in the correct firing position. Anything less means that you do not have complete control of the pistol and in all probability will fire an inaccurate shot. For this vitally important reason, it is recommended that anyone intent on mastering the fast draw begin with an unloaded weapon and repeatedly make the draw in slow motion.

Concentrate on each step: sweep arm up and forward; grasp pistol and pull; insert finger in trigger guard; lock arm in firing position; hesitate to ensure alignment on target; squeeze through the trigger. Only when you feel confident that you can perform the draw smoothly and without mishap, which might require a hundred or more slow motion draws, should you advance to increased speed.

Still with an unloaded gun, execute the draw at half speed for a while, then with increasing rapidity, consciously focusing each time on completing the series of movements without flaw. While practicing, select some object as a target and concentrate thoroughly on attaining perfect, instinctive aim with each draw. One highly effective method of checking the aim is to draw facing a mirror, which will also provide the illusion of drawing against something. Over a period of time the reflection in the mirror will tend to occupy your mind, thus making the movements of the draw automatic, until finally they become an instinctive reaction. Never lose sight of the fact that the fast draw is merely a means to an end—placing the gun in a stable firing position in the shortest possible time. And one other thing—the most imperative element of all: consciously retain that fractionalized moment of hesitation to ensure deadly accuracy.

Eventually, each man reaches the point that he wants to test himself against elapsed time; possibly the most convenient means of doing so is to use a coin. Hold your gun arm straight forward at shoulder height and place a coin on top of the hand. Then drop your arm suddenly, complete the draw, and snap the trigger on a target before the coin reaches the ground. For the man of average height the elapsed time of this draw is approximately four-tenths of a second. In addition to improving speed, this exercise will also force you to perform draws with the hand somewhere other than hovering over the gun.

Another somewhat faster speed drill is to relax the gun arm at your side, holding the coin with your fingertips. Then release the coin and draw and simulate fire before the coin hits the ground. It should be noted that only the most skilled and highly coordinated will ever beat the coin with any regularity. The time involved is approximately one quarter of a second.

When the draw has been perfected to the point that it can be performed with smoothness at full speed, then you should begin practicing with the hand held in various awkward positions away from the pistol. Rarely, if ever, in a gunfight is a man permitted the luxury of standing poised and ready with his hand directly over the gun.

The draw should also be practiced while walking and in various situations where you are forced to spin left, right or completely about in order to face the target. If there is anyone available to act as a starter, it is extremely effective to have that person surprise you by yelling DRAW! The exercise forces you to instinctively complete the movements without forewarning or excessive mental preparation.

It cannot be stressed too strongly, however, to *be sure* that the pistol is *unloaded* when practicing any of the speed drills outlined above. Vast numbers of people have been killed with weapons thought to be unloaded. Only the foolhardy would practice the fast draw without first *double-checking* to assure themselves that the gun contains no live ammunition.

The fast draw is of value only to the accurate shooter. In a gunfight no one will be overawed by speed alone, and certainly speed in itself has never been known to neutralize an antagonist. The man who relies primarily on his fast draw, thereby relegating accuracy to second place, is a born loser. On the other hand, the man who perceives the fast draw in a supporting role to accuracy has a better than even chance of emerging unscathed from a gunfight with even the most desperate adversary.

When contemplating the situations one might encounter in terms of location, lack of warning and a man's position in relation to his opponent, the possibilities are almost infinite. There are a few generalized thoughts, however, which the man concerned with self-defense would do well to keep in mind:

The homeowner awakened by a noise in the middle of the night invariably switches on the bedroom light. This not only makes him a visible target but also has the immediate effect of blinding him to the darkness while leaving the intruder with night vision intact. In this situation you would retain an advantage by silently making your way to the source of the noise in the dark, then switch on a flashlight (holding it forward and to the extreme left in case the intruder should fire at the light).

It is also well to remember that in the dark or in dim light there is a tendency to shoot high, which means that the point of aim should be lower than it appears visually. Along this same vein, when shooting on a downward angle, such as down a flight of stairs, most men tend to shoot high. Conversely, if firing on an upward angle they tend to shoot low. Obviously then your point of aim should be adjusted to meet the situation. In total darkness the likelihood of firing at a sound and scoring a hit is also quite remote unless you're using a shotgun. The better approach is to wait until the intruder is silhouetted against a window or light-colored wall. Or else throw an object so that he will fire at the noise; then aim slightly to the right of the muzzle flash.

A brief aside: If you have children, be extremely cautious with firearms, especially pistols. A small child in the house is perhaps the best reason imaginable to own a shotgun for home defense. Specifically, a double-barrel shotgun can be kept unloaded but close at hand in the bedroom. In an emergency, it requires only a couple of seconds to load the weapon; otherwise the shells are locked away, safe from small, prying hands. If you are determined to have a pistol—with children in the house—then I suggest you buy an automatic. The loaded magazine can be kept hidden, or locked away, until an emergency arises. Then you simply slam the magazine into the pistol butt, jerk the slide back, and you're in business. Total elapsed time, including digging out the hidden magazine, would be less than thirty seconds, which is a petty inconvenience indeed if it ensures the safety of your children. Trigger locks are also an excellent way to child-proof a pistol. But again, I would advise you—for the multitude of reasons previously stated—to buy yourself a shotgun!

Now, back to the action and another tip that might save your life. *Never run to a gunfight!* Short breath and a shaky hand will invariably throw your shots wild. Unless you hear screams (or other signs that someone is in mortal danger), then force yourself to walk fast and take deep breaths to steady your nerves. If you are unable to exercise regularly, then at the very least buy a couple of small rubber balls in the variety store. (The type used by children; cost approximately 35¢ each.) Squeeze the balls with both hands a minimum of one-hundred times a day and you'll be pleasantly surprised. The strength of your grip will become solid; your forearms muscular, and your gun hand will lock on a pistol like a vise. It's a simple exercise (often overlooked for that very reason) but it might well guarantee you a steady hand when the chips are down.

As an example, there's always the possibility that you will be faced either in your home or on the street by two or more armed assailants. The margin for survival in such a predicament is deliberate accuracy. Once accosted, you should fire first at the man to the direct front or on the right, since this requires the least body movement in order to align the shot. Only after firing *two shots* at anyone on your front or right side, should you spin and confront the adversary on your left. When faced by opponents who are standing at various distances away, your initial fire should be directed at the nearest man, since the assailant farthest away will be more likely to miss with his opening shots.

When your attacker is running laterally across the line of vision, then it must be taken into consideration that a shot fired directly at a running man will strike behind him. That being the case, it is necessary to lead, or fire just in front of him, so that the slug and the running man reach the same point at the same time. Generally, a shot placed a foot in front of a running man at any range within thirty yards will score a hit, even though he might only be wounded. When confronted with opponents running toward or away from you at close ranges, then you should fire as if they were standing directly in front of you, since their running movement doesn't materially change the point of aim.

In a situation with the assailant to your rear, you must gauge the man's location by any sound or movement, then whirl in the direction which requires minimum turn to align the gun for a shot. Clearly, if the attacker were to your left rear, then spinning to the right could be a fatal mistake. This would require a body movement consuming almost twice the time it would have taken for a turn to the left.

Just as you practiced to achieve accuracy and speed on the draw, so you would be well advised to familiarize yourself with gunfight situations firing both pellets and live ammunition. Silhouette targets can initially be erected in the backyard or garage so that various body movements and readjustment in aim become apparent while firing the pellet pistol. When spinning to face a new direction—while at the same time attempting to draw, align the gun, come to rest in a solid shooting stance, and fire accurately—a man finds there are just too many things to think about if he is consciously trying to execute and coordinate all of these actions simultaneously. The body movement must be worked out in advance, just as the draw and alignment of the gun were practiced, if the two elements are to ever be fused as one into an instantaneous reaction. Practice and more practice, sometimes many hours of it, will be necessary for the man of normal physical coordination before he will be able to combine body movement with shooting accuracy.

Basically, there are four movements, each of which involve pivoting of the feet. Until these pivots are perfected, the remainder of the movement will continue to be clumsy. When turning to the right, the pivot must be made on the right foot while the left foot is swung around and planted solidly at the point the turn is to be completed. If the turn is to the left, then the procedure is reversed, with the left foot being used for the pivot. When spinning in a complete turn to the right rear, then the left foot is used for the pivot while the right foot is swung in an arc and firmly planted as a means of halting the spin. If the spin is to the left rear, then the right foot must be used for the pivot and the left foot as a brake to stop the movement on target.

Initially, these movements should be practiced with the pellet pistol held down at your side when the turn or spin is begun. After whatever period of time is necessary to perfect the movement, and alignment of the gun on target, then you can actually begin firing the pellet pistol in an effort to combine accuracy with movement. Gradually, as you learn to coordinate movement with accuracy, you can progress to two and then three silhouette targets. Any number of target situations can be arranged to test reaction time and skill. One target to the front and one to either side; one each at front and right side and another to the left rear; one five yards to the front, another ten yards to the left front and the last ten yards to the direct rear. The combinations are endless, and each time the challenge of a new one is met and mastered, you are a step closer to being able to handle any situation you might encounter. It should be noted that realistic skills have not been attained until you can unfailingly place two shots in the chest-stomach area of each silhouette regardless of the target combination that has been arranged.

By climbing up on a ladder (and shooting down) or nailing a target to a rafter in the garage (and shooting up), it is even possible to gain perspective as to point of aim at varied elevations. For practice on running objects, it is excellent to attach a framed silhouette target to a moving type clothesline and have someone run it back and forth across the lateral line of vision. Head-on practice on moving objects can be accomplished in the same manner by standing at one end of the clothesline and having someone run the silhouette back and forth, which very effectively simulates the jerky motions of a running man. The great advantage of a pellet pistol is that you can practice daily and inexpensively, even though you may be unable to live fire at a range except on weekends.

Ultimately, you will develop sufficient confidence to begin firing live ammunition in conjunction with the fast draw, turns and spins, and other situations involved in a total approach to gunfighting. When that time arrives, maintain *constant awareness* that the gun you hold is a lethal weapon whether it is fired accidentally or purposely. Many men have had legs and hip sockets shattered by slugs simply because they moved into fast-draw live fire without adequate simulated practice. Like any skill which challenges a man's physical and mental coordination, rapid fire accuracy with a gun demands constant practice, and intense concentration at all times. The man who plans to give it anything less had best learn to turn the other cheek—or else take up sprinting as a means of self-defense.

Finally, for the man who intends to master the gun as a means of protecting life and property, there is the timeless advice to learn the difference between *fast* and *quick*. Since the advent of Samuel Colt's Equalizer, and gunfighting as an American phenomenon, there have been many men who drew fast and shot fast. Then there were the others who drew just as fast, but shot only quickly. From this enduring contest we can observe the grim lesson of the Quick and the Dead.

The five inflexible rules for survival in a gunfight:

1. Never attempt to bluff with a gun. While you are hesitating and talking, your assailant can and will kill you.

2. Never shoot to wound. Your assailant remains dangerous as long as he can grip a gun. While you are practicing humanity, he can and will kill you.

3. When faced with an armed assailant, hold your fire only if the situation has permitted you to get the drop on him, and you are assured of being able to fire the first shot should he make the slightest move.

4. Once you begin shooting, don't stop until your assailant is either disarmed or neutralized. Should you cease firing simply because your antagonist is hit, he can and will kill you.

5. Regardless of the slugs coming your way, summon up the nerve to hesitate for that fraction of a second required to fire each shot with deliberate accuracy.

5

KNIFE FIGHTING

Gold is for the mistress—silver for the maid
Copper for the craftsman cunning at his trade.
'Good!' said the Baron, sitting in his hall,
'But Iron—Cold Iron—is master of them all.'
—Rudyard Kipling

A Knife Fight is Dirty Business

IT'S MESSY and dangerous, and the end result often weakens even the strongest stomach. Since Stone Age Man first learned to sharpen flint, however, humans have been using knives to defend themselves. Throughout all of recorded history, the simple blade has remained the one indispensable weapon of every culture, no matter how advanced or primitive it be. Archaeologists have unearthed knives from virtually every continent around the globe; the pattern of development has been traced from the copper daggers of ancient Egypt to the true iron-bladed fighting knife crafted by the Hittites. Yet, contrary to legend, there is neither romance nor honor attached to knife fighting.

Late in the 15th Century the French referred to their deadly battle knife as *couteaux de brèche,* which rather succinctly illustrates the point. Always pragmatic about such matters, man has simply found a well-honed blade to be one of the swiftest and most expedient means of dispatching his enemies to the next world. It carves and cuts and spills buckets of blood. Far messier than a gunshot wound, its butchering effect is hardly a pretty sight. But it's handy and silent, an efficient killing tool, and perhaps the most fearsome form of combat ever devised by man.

In knife fighting, victory belongs to the fast, aggressive individual who can nervelessly face a foot of cold steel. Yet the effect on the psyche of men confronted by a knife is often demoralizing, if not debilitating. Those who have entered the circle of death—the radius of a few feet separating two knife-wielding antagonists—have found it to be one of the most intimidating experiences in life. Since the number of men who would willingly provoke such an ordeal has always been small, the knife remains essentially a weapon of self-defense.

This psychological inhibitor seems to be a universal trait, even among those cultures where the art of knife fighting is practiced from childhood. *It is a rare man who can face cold steel with the same equanimity that he would fire a gun or strike with his fist.* Psychiatrists would doubtless interpret this as a manifestation of man's subconscious fear of castration. Certainly, for anyone who has ever had a blade flicked in the immediate proximity of his groin, the fear ceases to be subliminal and becomes quite real. Of course, from a more practical standpoint, it comes down to the fact that in a knife fight *you* are literally staring death in the face. There are few men capable of displaying normal composure when they become that intimate with mortality.

Still, there are exceptions. James Bowie, who killed numerous men with his legendary bowie knife, was one of an extraordinary breed who preferred the blade to less personal weapons. Without exaggeration, it might be stated that Bowie exulted in the circle of death. So fully in fact that he once instigated a knife fight in which he and his adversary straddled a log facing one another and then had themselves nailed by the pants to their bizarre arena. Not surprisingly, Bowie carved his opponent into bite-sized chunks.

Such men have a peculiar, almost aberrant, obsession with the knife as an instrument of their wrath. In the main, however, they represent only a small contingent among the many who have been forced to defend themselves with a blade. The homeowner or man on the street who suddenly finds himself in a knife fight should anticipate that he will experience an instinctive, overpowering fear. It is equally probable that his assailant will be afflicted with the same emotions, even though he might hide them beneath a superficial aggressiveness. Of course, there are no guarantees.

The streets of America today are filled with drug addicts and psychos and amoral crazies. Not long ago, a paroled mental patient ambushed the neighborhood beat cop with a butcher knife and killed him. It happened in New York, but it might well have occurred in Anytown, U.S.A. The incident captured headlines—instead of being buried on the obituary page—only because the victim was an *armed* cop. With minor variations, similar attacks on *unarmed* citizens occur at the rate of one a minute! Day after day, regular as clockwork, it happens year round across the nation.

The crucial factor in any such confrontation is not fear itself, but rather in how you *control* that fear. Blind panic will get you killed. The sight of cold steel will almost certainly jangle your nerves. So accept that, and be prepared for the reaction. Before you can control the action in a knife fight, and neutralize your assailant, you must first control yourself. By dominating your fear—converting that surge of adrenalin into disciplined anger—you will have taken the first step in dominating the fight. Knowledge of knife-fighting techniques (and practice in the subtleties of cold steel) will bolster your confidence. But unless you can move into the circle of death with *controlled fear,* then you are advised to run like hell.

So there you have the cardinal rule of knife fighting. Either dominate your fear or else put a lot of distance between yourself and the other fellow.

Before proceeding further, perhaps a brief look at the legal ramifications would be in order. Laws which forbid carrying concealed weapons are fairly uniform throughout the United States. Generally these laws include sheath knives or even pocket knives with unusally long blades. Nearly all cities and states, however, have no law prohibiting possession of a pocket knife if the blade is 4″ or less. Such knives are commonly referred to as a Jackknife or a Folding Hunter; with their wide blade and finely honed edge, they are indisputably lethal. Jackknives do require precious seconds to flip open the blade. There is a further hazard that the lock mechanism will fail when the blade strikes bone; the blade then folds back, severing finger tendons, and the knife slips from your crippled hand. It makes for a dicey situation.

The same thought applies to the lock mechanism on a switchblade. Worse, it is illegal *everywhere* to be caught carrying a switchblade. So you would be wise to avoid the faithful old stiletto altogether. Still, any knife is better than no knife at all, especially if turning the other cheek goes against the grain. At the very least, get yourself a Folding Hunter manufactured by a reliable knifemaker. It's legal, and on a dark street it might just save your life.

True fighting knives, of course, are by definition sheath knives. The longer blade provides the maximum advantage as a self-defense weapon, and when kept in the home or carried on a hunting/camping/fishing trip, these knives are perfectly legal. While I *do not* recommend it, I personally have no qualms about carrying a concealed fighting knife in high crime areas. This is particularly true in major cities with harsh gun laws and epidemic street crime. Bluntly stated, I would rather be alive and facing a jury than the deceased *unarmed victim* of a street thug. That's strictly my personal philosophy, however, and in no way is it meant to encourage others to do likewise. The law is explicit in *most* cities, and anyone who carries a fighting knife does so at his own risk.

The law notwithstanding, there are many excellent fighting knives available in sporting goods stores. These knives are factory produced, but they are generally made of fine steel and are relatively low priced. Two of the most popular (and also the most deadly) are replicas of the Bowie Knife and the Fairbairn-Sykes Commando Knife used in World War II. Although moderately expensive, handmade fighting knives are available from several custom knifemakers around the country. As thousands of servicemen will attest, the Randall Company of Orlando, Florida probably makes the finest fighting knife ever manufactured in the United States. Some of these handmade knives are so wicked in appearance that the mere presence of one is often sufficient to deter a would-be mugger/rapist/robber.

A brief aside to illustrate the value of deterrence. On many occasions I have forestalled violence simply by flashing a fighting knife. Late one wintry night in New

York, after visiting a friend, I was standing on the corner of Fifth Avenue and 103rd Street trying to flag a cab. Out of the snow flurries appeared a powerfully built man, striding briskly in the direction of Harlem. The street was deserted, and as he passed by, he gave me a quick once over. Then he suddenly whirled around, less than ten feet separating us, and started toward me. In the parlance of the street, we both knew where it was at.

I reached inside my coat and pulled a Commando Knife. He stopped cold, watching me intently. Perhaps he was armed, perhaps he wasn't. I never found out. The distance had narrowed to a couple of steps, and we both knew I could get him before he got me. After a moment he smiled, then shook his head, and took off at a fast clip toward Harlem. Since he had me shaded by six inches and probably fifty pounds, the story would have had a different ending except for the deterrent effect of the knife.

On another occasion, I was camped with my wife along a river in the mountain wilderness of a National Park. Shortly before sundown, we were startled by three fishermen crashing through the brush toward our campsite. The men reeked of whiskey, and each of them had a pint bottle stuck in his hip pocket. We swapped pleasantries, discussing the fishing prospects, but after a few minutes' conversation, the men seemed disinclined to move on. One of them offered us a drink, and I noticed the other two exchange a furtive glance. It was perhaps the only time I have ever regretted my wife's good looks; none of the men could keep his eyes off her. In the remoteness of those mountains, miles from any lawman, we were suddenly confronted with the potential of a very ugly situation.

While firearms are prohibited in National Parks, I had strapped on my belt an Arkansas Toothpick. The knife resembles a small broadsword; one look would convince anyone as to its purpose. I pulled the knife, backed to a tree, and casually clipped a low hanging branch. Then I began removing the foliage with effortless little flicks of the blade. In a sense, the message was razor sharp, and within moments, our uninvited guests had departed. Perhaps they were simply drunk and meant no harm and wanted some one to share their bottle. Or perhaps they had stumbled across something they wanted more. I don't know, and under the circumstances, I had no intention of testing their motives. Odds of three to one, particularly in the wilderness, aren't conducive to fair play. The fact remains, I had the knife and indicated a willingness to use it. The three fishermen (whatever they had on their minds) took the hint and hastily set off downriver. And my wife slept a lot easier that night.

Like a gun or a club or any other true weapon, the knife is a persuasive deterrent in a violent situation. The key is your mental attitude. A potential assailant must *believe* that you are prepared and willing to use the knife. If you aren't, then pulling the knife could start a fight in which you are psychologically whipped even before the action begins. The sole reason violence was forestalled in the situations above was because the individuals involved knew I *would* use the knife if pressed. Space permitting, I could relate several incidents where the deterrent effect failed and it became necessary to use the knife. So remember, a knife fight has nothing whatever in common with the game of poker. Don't bluff! If you pull a knife, make damned sure you're prepared to use it.

All of which brings us to the initial step for those who have decided to master the art of knife fighting. Simple as it sounds, you must select a knife. Yet it is hardly a selection to be made lightly. In an emergency, you might rely on the family butcher knife or your trusty hunting knife or even a small steak knife. On the other hand, any of those knives would result in a nasty outcome if you went

Figure 1. Fighting Knives. (1) Fairbairn-Sykes Commando Knife. (2) Rigid Arkansas Toothpick. (3) Randall Model 2 with fighting hilt. (*Author's collection.*)

up against a skilled opponent who was using a true fighting knife.

There are divergent schools of thought on what constitutes the optimum fighting knife. Some men swear by the Bowie Knife. Others are devoted to the military KA-BAR or similar hybrids currently produced by custom knifemakers. Personally, I favor the dagger design, which provides a cutting edge along the entire length of *both* sides of the blade. (Three knives of the dagger design are illustrated in *Fig. 1.)* The advantages of a double-edged blade will be discussed in the section dealing with knife fighting technique. Whichever blade design you ultimately select, handle a number of knives before you decide. The heft and that intangible *feel* are vital factors. A large measure of confidence will stem from the inner belief that the knife you chose has the right blade for *you.*

NOTE: Perhaps it sounds redundant, but the thought bears repeating: In knife fighting, there is no such thing as overkill. Use the maximum knife you can skillfully handle in a combat situation. The custom-made Arkansas Toothpick illustrated in *Fig. 1* weighs two pounds and has a blade 10″ long. It is a special design, fashioned on the old Roman shortsword, and measures 15″ from butt to point. Some men would consider it cumbersome and unwieldy, far more knife than is needed to get the job done. Looking across that blade in a knife fight, however, those same men would wish to hell they had a pig-sticker of equal size. Assuming comparable skills in two knife fighters, the man with the optimum blade will invariably walk away the winner. So take your time and select all the knife you can comfortably manage.

Of course, there are any number of variables that could influence your selection. In a city with restrictive laws, you might be limited *legally* to a Jackknife or a Folding Hunter. Or perhaps you would prefer a belt buckle knife (illustrated in *Fig. 2*) which is something of a hideout weapon and guaranteed to startle even the most jaded mugger. Another choice would be a small boot knife (generally with a blade 5″ or less) which is easily concealed and available from several custom knifemakers. If cost is a factor, then you could hardly do better than a replica Fairbairn-Sykes Commando Knife (illustrated in *Fig. 1*) which usually sells for $15.00 or less. Avoid exotic weapons, however, such as the old Trench knife or the Kris or the Gurkha. Not only are these knives illegal in most cities, but they have proved to be dismal failures except as weapons of assassination.

The wisest course is to visit several sporting goods stores and handle a number of knives. Also, keep in mind, if you can afford forty or fifty dollars for a factory produced knife, then you are well within the price range of a great many custom fighting knives. The base price on

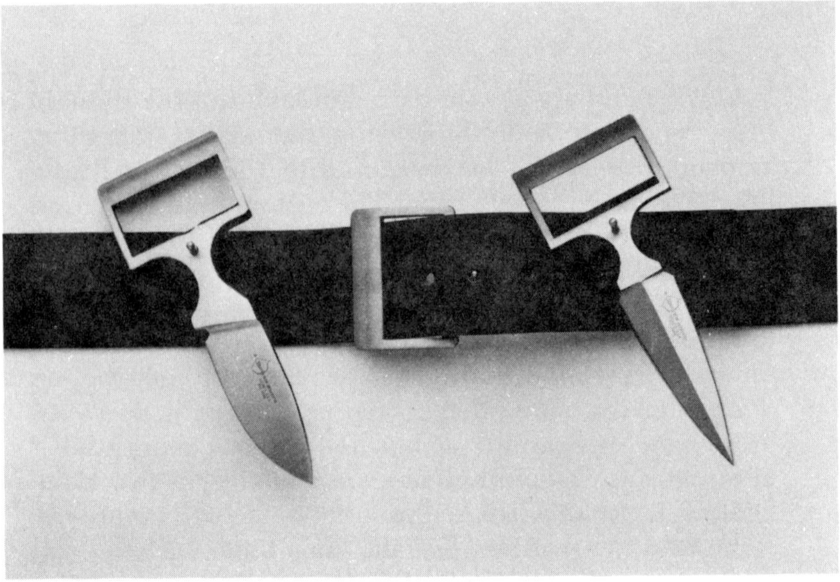

Figure 2. Belt Buckle Knife. Bowen Survivor Belt with buckle knife. (1) Single Edge Model #109. (2) Double Edge Model #105. (*Photo courtesy Bowen Knife Company.*)

a handmade Randall Model 2 (illustrated in *Fig. 1*) is comparable to what you would pay for a top-of-the-line store-bought knife. Order the catalogues of a few custom knifemakers before you make the final selection. There are knives and there are *knives,* and you might be pleasantly surprised to find that you can have the best for only a few dollars more.

Once you have selected a knife that has good heft and fits comfortably in a firm grip, then the blade must be sharpened to a finely honed edge. The skilled knife fighter rarely ever *thrusts* with a blade, and if he expects to live very long, he never uses it with either an overhead or an upper stabbing motion. Thus we are led to the conclusion that knife fighting consists primarily of a series of forward and backward slashing cuts. Obviously, when the object is to slash one's opponent with the edge of the blade, then that edge must be as close to razor sharp as possible. In the case of a double-edged knife, which provides the advantage of either a forward or a backward slash without rotating the wrist, then both sides of the blade must be sharpened.

Commercial whetstones are available in almost any sporting goods store; with only a little practice, you should be able to remove the rough edge common to most factory knives and bring the blade to something approaching true sharpness. Once the whetstone has been placed on a flat surface, such as a table, then the knife edge should be laid on the stone with the blade turned sideways at approximately a twenty degree angle. The blade is then drawn backward in a circular, sweeping motion across the stone for three or four strokes. The opposite edge is then placed on the stone and the procedure repeated. Within a matter of minutes, the two sides of the blade will begin to form a single, sharpened edge, which can be tested by lightly running the underside of the thumb down the blade. If the skin is cut then the knife is sharp enough for virtually any engagement. The individual who wishes an even finer edge can easily acquire a leather strop, such as those used by barbers; after using the whetstone, then strop the blade as a finishing touch.

The essential, of course, regardless of the sharpening method employed, is that the knife have a keen cutting edge. Without it, the man involved in a knife fight might as well try cutting steak with an ice cream scoop.

Still, even with a razor-sharp knife, a man must know the primary targets—where to cut—before he undertakes fighting technique itself. Fortunately, Major W. E. Fairbairn, codesigner of the famed Commando Knife, left us with invaluable, wartime documentation concerning body areas most vulnerable to knife attack. Fairbairn very astutely perceived that in the heat of a knife fight certain vital, life-supporting areas are more *accessible* than others. Strictly from a tactical standpoint, he designated six primary target areas. While I disagree with elements of Fairbairn's theory (because certain body areas are, in fact, tactically *inaccessible*), it is worthwhile to analyze his findings point by point.

1. *The Heart.* Located behind a mass of bone and muscle, the heart is an extremely difficult target to reach. It requires a thrust of considerable force, either beneath the breastbone or through the rib cage, to penetrate the 4–5 inches of flesh protecting the heart. A direct strike (which would cause near instantaneous death) is a chancey proposition at best in a swift-moving knife fight. Moreover, the thrust position itself (unless your opponent's knife arm has been neutralized) will leave you vulnerable to immediate counterattack. Even worse, if you miss the heart, and your knife lodges in that mass of bone and muscle, you may come away empty-handed. A deep stab wound has a tendency to contract around the blade; it might take both hands and considerable tugging to withdraw your knife. It's strictly a toss of the dice, so save that heart thrust for your *coup de grâce.*

2. *The Subclavian Artery.* Located along the collarbone, this artery is virtually impossible to attack with any degree of accuracy. Perhaps a battle axe or a broadsword would do the trick, but if you try it in a knife fight, you'll likely step back with your throat slit. A subclavian cut becomes practical only when your opponent is disabled. Even then, there are targets better suited for the final blow.

3. *The Stomach.* The abdominal aorta is located some 4–5 inches beneath the surface of the skin. A slashing cut (which *will* produce shock) rarely penetrates to the depth

of this artery. It requires a deep stabbing thrust, generally followed by a cross-ripping motion of the blade, to sever the abdominal aorta. All of that takes a bit of doing, and leaves you dangerously exposed to your opponent's knife. However, the stomach is an excellent target for slashing cuts, and one well-directed blow can easily cripple an adversary. Also, as previously mentioned, the stomach is in close proximity to the groin, and any slash in the immediate vicinity will give the other fellow's psyche a real workout.

4. *The Brachial Artery.* A fairly accessible artery which supplies muscular branches of the upper arm. Usually it is easiest cut across the inner arm directly above the elbow. In a knife fight, this particular artery (on both the knife arm and the left arm) is frequently exposed and vulnerable to attack. The brachial artery is *highly* susceptible to attack if the slash is preceded by a feint. If the artery is completely severed, loss of consciousness will occur within a minute and death will result shortly thereafter. It is a key target, and should be attacked at every opportunity.

5. *The Radial Artery.* Located on top the forearm, this artery follows along the radius, which is the arm bone directly in line with the thumb. The artery branches off in several directions: to the elbow joint; to the wrist joint; to the thumb; and to the index finger. It offers a veritable grab bag of disabling cuts; because of surrounding tendons and nerves, even a superficial cut on the knife arm will force an opponent to drop his knife. The artery is closest to the skin along the wrist, and if severed completely, death occurs within minutes. In a knife fight, the forearm is perhaps the most vulnerable part of the entire body; use of the proper feint will create opportunities for a cut to either the knife arm or the left arm. The radial ar-

tery is a major target, and should be attacked with concerted effort throughout the fight.

6. *The Carotid Artery.* Commonly associated with the jugular vein, this artery extends along the side of the neck and controls brain function as well as the larynx and the windpipe. It is *extremely* accessible to the skilled knife fighter, since it can be attacked from virtually any position with either a forward or a backward slash. Under the right circumstances, it can also be severed with a well-directed thrust. By employing any one of several feints, the knife fighter can fake his opponent into an exposed position and deliver a cleanly executed cut to the carotid artery. The wonder of this particular cut is that it will end the fight within a few heartbeats; death occurs almost instantaneously. Even a near miss effectively terminates the fight: a damaging cut to the larynx (Adam's apple) or the trachea (windpipe) results in immediate shock and/or death. The neck is vulnerable at *all* times during a knife fight, and the carotid artery is the *prime* target on the entire body. A calculated and concerted attack should be directed at the throat from the very outset of any engagement.

These are the six major target areas designated by Major W. E. Fairbairn. But they are by no means the *only* target areas, nor are they always readily accessible when pitted against a skilled opponent. An experienced knife fighter is both pragmatic and realistic, otherwise he would never have lived to gain the experience. As a result, he enters an engagement not with any great expectation of killing his opponent immediately, but rather with the tactical plan of crippling his opponent—neutralizing the ability to retaliate—and then he delivers the final blow. In a sense, he whittles his opponent into submission; the vast majority of knife fights are won by the man who carves and slices and methodically destroys the other fellow's capacity to defend himself. Of course, the goal of every tactical move in a fight is to "set up" an instantaneous death blow. However, a skilled knife fighter never goes for the jugular unless he can do so without unwarranted danger to himself.

Thus, the pragmatic approach forms the basis of fighting technique, and leads to an apparent conclusion. There are several additional target areas which should become part and parcel of a knife fighter's repertoire. Briefly, these target areas can be categorized in general terms.

TARGETS OF OPPORTUNITY. Dismiss *nothing* as a potential target! The action in a knife fight is fast and furious, and at any given moment, countless parts of the body are exposed. Perhaps the cut (or thrust) will prove nonlethal, but at the very least it will intimidate your opponent, and it might well induce a momentary state of shock. A target of opportunity generally occurs when your opponent has attacked—unsuccessfully—but hasn't yet recovered his balance.

React instantly! Attack the nearest thing within reach. A lightning jab to the eyes, guaranteed to rattle anyone's nerves. A quick flick of your blade in his face: cut the cheek, forehead, mouth or ears and his boldness will take a nosedive. Deliver darting slashes to any part of the arms, chest, shoulders, hands or legs: even shallow cuts can destroy muscle, sever tendons and paralyze nerve centers. Prick him anywhere with the point of your blade; even the slightest jab will sting and momentarily focus his mind on the hurt rather than your next move.

The object of all this is to draw blood, punish him, intimidate him. All the while, of course, you remain alert for that *real* target of opportunity—the throat. Once his resistance is lowered, and he's fighting scared, you'll get your chance. Then you move, no hesitation. Fake him out of his jockstrap and end it.

SURPRISE TARGETS. The oldest adage in military tactics is to strike where least expected, the surprise attack! In personal combat, you must also capitalize on the element of surprise. Attack *unanticipated* targets, either by design or as the opportunity presents itself. Generally, an attack to a surprise target is most successful when your opponent is off balance or out of position. Obviously then, you can either lure him into a trap or else fake one way and go the other. The object is to take him off guard, strike where he least expects it.

Feint high, then duck low, and slash to the inside of the thigh. The femoral artery is directly below the groin, located on the inside of the thigh; a forceful slash will sever the artery completely, and bring on death within a couple of minutes. At worst, assuming you miss the artery, the damaged thigh muscles will severely hobble your opponent throughout the remainder of the fight.

Another tip: never overlook the lowly armpit! On occasion, particularly if you circle clockwise and then suddenly dart counterclockwise, your opponent will reflexively raise his left arm. Cut him under the armpit—the last thing he'd expect—and you will sever the axillary artery. Death will occur in approximately thirty seconds. If you're nimble and quick, then you can really get tricky. Suck your opponent into an attack, then duck low and slip past him on either side. (To your left if his knife arm is extended; to your right if his knife arm is retracted.) As you slide past, stab him low in the side and rip the blade backward into the kidney. Then leap clear and circle him, forcing him to keep moving. He'll fall in considerably less than a minute. Or if your opponent becomes careless (with either arm) merely slice him above and behind the elbow. It paralyzes the arm and severs the ulnar artery; death results in a couple of minutes.

Perhaps the purpose of focusing on surprise targets can best be illustrated by a brief aside. Years ago, when I was active in competitive épée fencing, I devised a series of feints which ended with a thrust to the groin. Although the groin is a legitimate target in épée, it was thought to be an "ungentlemanly" attack and was rarely employed. The tactic worked enormously well. It surprised my opponents, and won several matches I might otherwise have lost. The fact that gentlemen fencers considered it a "low blow" bothered me not at all. The object was to win, and I won! Any serious student of knife fighting will recognize this as another cardinal rule and adopt it as part of his personal code.

In knife fighting, second best is dead.

So fix these target areas firmly in your mind. Study them as if you were a surgeon analyzing vital body functions. Only when the primary targets evoke an instinctive reaction—require no conscious thought—are you capable of defending yourself. And in a very real sense, the life you save may be your own.

Before we proceed to fighting technique, however, there are several preliminary observations worth considering. Not unlike a gladiator of old, an individual must understand the rudiments of the craft before he progresses to combat tactics. On this foundation of basics, we will then advance step-by-step to the finesse of attack and counterattack.

THE RITUAL. There are varying schools of thought concerning the art of knife fighting. Broadly categorized, we find the European School, the Asian School and the American School (which seeks to combine the best of Oriental and Occidental). Unfortunately, a great part of the technique advocated is based on the science of an altogether different weapon, the sword. Several knife fighting "theorists" have introduced stylistic moves perfectly suited to the rapier; these same moves in a knife fight are an open invitation to sudden death. After some years of épée competition, as well as several engagements with the knife, I concluded that one has very little in common with the other. The techniques employed with three feet of steel in your hand are in no way applicable when you're holding a knife. Any veteran knife fighter, whether trained in back alleys or by the Special Forces, would make short work of theorists who attempt "thrust and parry" swordplay at close quarters. By way of illustration, let me say that I was cut twice before I learned the difference. I haven't been cut since.

Based on personal experience, and the experience of men I have trained, I urge you to forget the Three Musketeers and the Samurai. Your weapon is a knife, and its effective *strike zone* is roughly the length of your arm. Unlike the sword, every time you extend that knife, you are within your *opponent's* strike zone. Perhaps an old cliché will stress the message in a way that everyone can remember.

Fools walk in where angels fear to tread.

THE COMBAT GRIP. There are a number of ways to hold a knife. But there is only *one* way to grip a fighting knife. (Illustrated in *Fig. 3.*) Again, forget the rapier and the saber and the broadsword. Learn to hold the fighting knife correctly, and then practice that *one* grip until it becomes instinctive.

Lay the knife across your palm. The hilt should be parallel to your index finger and the blade parallel to your outstretched thumb. Now curl your fingers around the flat of the handle and lay your thumb along the top of the

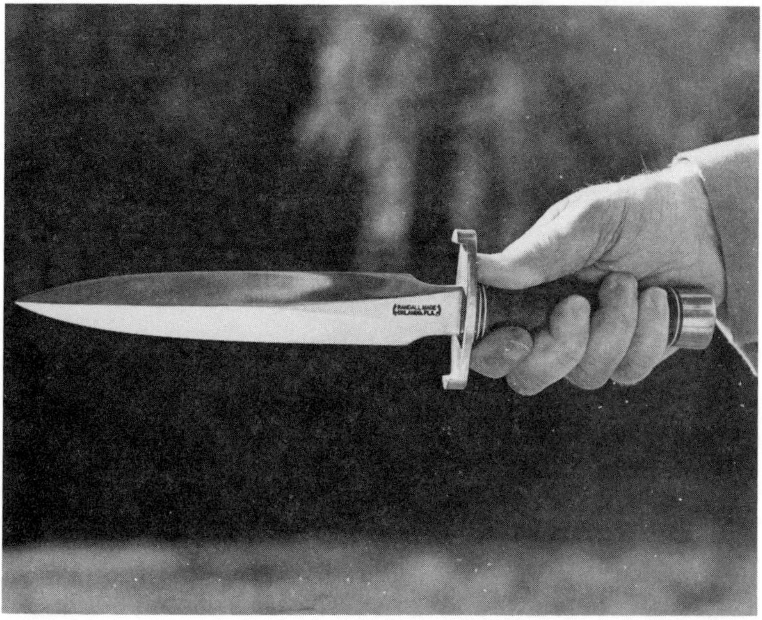

Figure 3.

handle. Then press your thumb forward against the back of the hilt and grasp the handle tightly with your fingers. Hold the knife with the flat of the blade roughly parallel to the ground (or cant the outside cutting edge downward about forty-five degrees), and finally, turn the point of the knife slightly inward, on a direct line with your opponent's left side. The theorists have tried for decades to improve on the Combat Grip, but none has succeeded. The reasons become self-evident in any serious engagement.

The Combat Grip provides maximum control of the blade and the ultimate in deft handling. You can flick, cut, slash or thrust from any position and never once have to change your grip. Moreover, this same grip allows you to execute both the forward cross slash and the backward slash without rotating either your wrist or the blade (assuming you use a double-edged knife). In a

Figure 4.

slash or thrust, you will also deliver optimum force behind the blow, which is vital when attacking heavily muscled targets. Finally, for those all-imperative cuts to hand tendons and arm veins, you can strike in any direction with the blade vertical or horizontal. In short, the limitations are practically nil and the advantages unsurpassed.

So don't experiment. Use the Combat Grip. It works.

THE COMBAT STANCE. The key to survival in a knife fight is agility and maneuverability. Like a boxer, the knife fighter moves with fluidity of motion, utilizing speed, deception and lightning reflexes. The man who has lead in his feet, or lacks quick reaction time, would do well to avoid any engagement with knives.

The basic Combat Stance (illustrated in *Fig. 4*) is both

the best defensive position and the most effective attack position. The torso is held erect, the knees bent in a slight crouch, and the head tucked back on a straight line with the chest. The legs are spread, with the weight evenly distributed on both feet; the left foot is positioned slightly forward of the body. The knife hand is partially extended, with the forearm slightly below chest level and parallel to the ground; the elbow is cocked and on line with the chest, and positioned a few inches away from the side. The left hand is extended forward, positioned for fending or grabbing, held at chest level with the palm toward the opponent. *NOTE:* Don't block a knife blow with your left hand unless there is no alternative. However, if you must be cut, then take the blow on the palm. You need that left hand in various counterattack situations, and a cut on the palm does less damage to tendons than a cut on the back of the hand.

The Combat Stance would offend devotees of the fencing foil or épée. In those highly stylized sports, the participants are trained to present the smallest possible target by turning sideways to their opponent. Within the infinitely smaller radius of a knife fight, however, the frontal stance allows instant maneuverability in any direction. From this position, the individual can move to either side, or backward and forward with equal ease. Moreover, with the weight stabilized on both feet, it enables a man to deliver slash, cut or thrust without additional body movement. In a sustained attack, involving a series of blows, the individual can easily advance one step at a time if his opponent retreats. But even then, with the legs spread and the weight evenly distributed, balance and freedom of movement are retained in the Combat Stance.

Generally, the wisest tactic in a knife fight is to circle to the left, as this allows the left hand to act as a shield while the knife hand is positioned to attack or counterattack. Also, moving to the left will place the left foot slightly in advance of the right, which expedites stepping forward with the left leg when initiating a sustained attack. If the attack fails, it is then quicker (with the right foot anchored) to shift backward into a defensive stance. In certain counterattacks, it is also necessary to step forward on the left leg; once again, moving in that direction, with the left foot already in the lead, expedites the blow. Since the Combat Stance adapts itself to this basic circling tactic, you have yet another reason to accept it as the prime knife-fighting position.

Of course the critical factor, overshadowing all else, is maneuverability. Never commit yourself to *one* pattern of movement. Stay fluid at all times; mix your moves in an unpredictable pattern. Circle left, then suddenly reverse yourself and circle right. Quickly dart in and out; feint and deliver a blow, or feint and sucker your opponent into a clumsy attack. Then counterattack! The idea is to retain your own mobility while forcing the other fellow into an awkward position. If your moves are swift and decisive, then he has no choice but to follow where you lead. This effectively roots him to the ground; keeps him off balance and uncertain, and forces him to assume a defensive posture. Now you have the initiative, and he's got a very big problem.

The Combat Stance wins knife fights. So don't improvise. Practice until you've mastered it, and then put it all together with the tactics of attack and counterattack.

THE THRUST. Properly executed, the thrust is an effective blow. Within the context of a knife fight, however, the thrust is merely an adjunct to the slash and the cut. Its primary value is as a feint—unless your opponent's knife arm has been neutralized—then it can be utilized to end the fight. Of course, the thrust does have its moments, particularly in counterattack. Yet even then, it puts you inside your opponent's strike zone, and you risk the chance of retaliation. In short, the thrust is a chancey proposition, and should be employed with vast caution.

To obtain deep penetration, the thrust must be delivered with considerable force. This necessitates one of two movements: either you get close enough to drive home the blade, or else you extend your arm and put the weight of your body behind the blow. The first method is merely risky. The second leaves you off balance, out of position, and vulnerable to immediate counterattack. In fact, it's one of those clumsy moves you should sucker an opponent into attempting. While he's hanging in midair, with his knife arm dangerously extended, you can whittle him down to size.

The extended arm thrust cannot be delivered to a vital area, with sufficient force, unless you expose yourself to your opponent's knife. The one exception is the throat. But the blow must be lightning fast, and you must withdraw immediately to a defensive stance. Otherwise, the extended arm thrust should be used only as a feint or as a crippling blow.

Unfortunately, the extended arm thrust has been advocated by theorists who borrowed heavily from the sport of fencing. To compound matters, the theorists have adopted highly stylized fencing maneuvers such as *Stocatta* and *Passata Sotto.* The former move, *Stocatta,* requires that you hold your ground, allow your opponent's blade to pass over your shoulder, and then stick him in the ribs. How you avoid his backward slash (since your blow will not kill him instantly) is one of the great mysteries of all time. The latter move, *Passata Sotto,* is even more incredible. You duck under an opponent's blow, dropping to one knee and lunging all at the same time, and thrust to the stomach. Then you try like hell to avoid his backward slash. Lots of luck!

If you have a very large death wish, then try one of these moves in a knife fight. Against a skilled adversary, it offers the near certainty that you will come away with a case of "instant slit throat." The reasons are patently obvious. You have exposed yourself to a lethal blow—sacrificing balance and mobility—in order to wound your opponent. It works in fencing because the action stops when the referee yells *"touché!"* In a knife fight, no matter how severely you wound your opponent, you won't be around to watch him fall. You'll be dead.

So leave the theory, and all that poetry in motion, to the ivory tower crowd. Get your mind down in the gutter, where the realism of knife fighting belongs. Think of the thrust as one of the minor options in your arsenal of tricks. Use it to feint. Use it to wound. Use it to intimidate. But don't use it to end the fight unless the danger to yourself is virtually eliminated.

And even then, be swift and be careful!

ATTACK AND COUNTERATTACK. There are no absolutes within the circle of death. Anything goes! The tactic that works, however unorthodox, is the tactic that will save your life. So look for the expedient and be damned pragmatic about the outcome. Your knife is quite literally a means to an end. Which brings us at last to the supreme cardinal rule:

Attack is the name of the game in knife fighting.

The individual who strikes first, moves the quickest and presses the attack aggressively is more often than not the man who walks away from an engagement with knives. It should also be stressed that in knife fighting, as in no other form of combat, a moving target is decidedly harder to hit. Therefore, an attacker must constantly circle his adversary, or move in and out as the flow of the fight dictates. Otherwise, he will rapidly find himself on the defensive, which is equivalent to a boxer being trapped in a corner of the ring. In this case, however, the conclusion would be of a rather permanent nature.

Since the object of any attack is to cut rather than stab an opponent, the priority of targets also bears repeating: throat and arms; stomach and face; legs and chest. Moreover, you must assume that an assailant remains dangerous until he has either been disarmed or eliminated. There are no alternatives! The fortitude and staying power of men pumped full of adrenalin during a fight is a fact duly recorded in the history of personal combat. Countless individuals have been wounded or crippled—even killed—by an adversary who had already absorbed inhuman punishment. The point is critical to your survival, so perhaps a grisly illustration will underscore the need to end a fight with dispatch and with finality.

In the lore of knife fighting, James Bowie stands as the classic example of the man who won't quit. On one occasion, knocked to the ground by multiple gunshot wounds, he was then skewered through the chest with a sword cane. Bowie grappled with his chief assailant, killing him instantly, and then charged the remaining henchmen with his infamous knife. A lurid account, written in the journalistic prose of the day, aptly describes the scene. "It was Bowie, terrible and bloody, scorning wounds, a steel shard protruding from his chest, yet striding in spite of a crippled leg, with berserk fury into the teeth of pistol fire. . . ." Not surprisingly, Bowie routed his enemies and lived to fight another day.

Some months later, ambushed in a wilderness canebrake, Bowie was again wounded by gunfire. His three assailants approached to finish the job, and within a matter of seconds, Bowie finished them. All were dispatched with the legendary knife. Which brings us back to the original premise.

There are men who simply never say die! Even wound-

Figure 5(A).

ed, their psychic tenacity is extraordinary; these are the men who will kill you unless you do the job right the first time. So don't hesitate, and don't go weak in the knees, and above all, don't develop a sudden fit of mercy. If you've been attacked with a knife, and somehow managed to defend yourself, then finish it. Or he'll finish you!

The art of knife fighting, as in most forms of close combat, requires that only a few basic tactics be mastered. Swift movement and fast-paced action demand an uncomplicated attack in which a series of blows are instinctively delivered in the correct sequence. Once the fundamentals have been acquired, then it remains only to perfect the movements and the speed with which they are executed. In perhaps the most elemental tactic (illustrated in *Fig. 5*), the attacker delivers a cross slash to his opponent's stomach *(A)*. If the opponent is agile enough to avoid the blow, then the attacker must immediately fol-

Figure 5(B).

low through with a crisp back slash directed at stomach level *(B)*. Should the opponent attempt to counterattack, after his evasive movement, then the back slash will catch him as he steps forward. On the other hand, if the opponent holds his position (and still evades the cross slash), then the attacker must retain the initiative. By executing a back slash to the stomach, he creates the potential for a sustained attack.

Once begun, the attack must be aggressively pressed. The quickest way to lose the initiative, which means you are immediately placed on the defensive, is to deliver only one blow and then hesitate instead of pushing forward with sustained slashes. Should the cross slash and the back slash in any given attack fail to strike the opponent, then the attacker still has an option. Depending on the situation, he can press the attack or return to the Combat Stance.

NOTE: A brief aside to define the proper execution of certain blows. The cross slash is delivered in a *short* sweeping arc; arm fully extended, with the point of the blade directed horizontally across your opponent's body. However, unless the blow connects, then the sweep of the blade *must be halted* as it passes your opponent's belt buckle. Otherwise, with your arm extended in a complete arc, you are off balance and vulnerable to immediate counterattack. The back slash, which *instantly* follows any cross slash, is executed by snapping the arm backward in a crisp, lightning-fast motion. Depending on your opponent's position, the back slash can be delivered horizontally to the stomach; or on an upward diagonal angle to the hands/arms/chest/throat/face; or on a downward diagonal angle to the hands/arms/groin/legs. In contrast, the cut type blow is executed with a quick slicing motion, either horizontally or vertically, and generally directed at the hands or arms. The wrist and forearm provide the force behind a cut; the blow is executed with a swift flick of the blade, without fully extending the arm. On occasion, the cut can be delivered to other parts of the body, principally the throat. However, the opportunity for such cuts usually occurs when *you* have evaded attack, and thus should be used as a rapid, slicing blow in counterattack.

The cross slash to the stomach is the most basic attack maneuver. The midriff presents the largest and the most tempting target; a slash through the abdominal wall produces, at the very least, a disabling wound. The stomach is so inviting a target, in fact, that the majority of men seem driven to concentrate their attack on that area. Understandably, just as most men engaged in hand-to-hand combat instinctively defend against a kick to the groin, so the man subjected to a knife fight will consciously protect his stomach. This defensive attitude is universal, and

Figure 6(A).

so compelling that it provides the perfect opening for diversionary tactics. The individual daring enough to capitalize on the situation can very decisively use the cross slash to the stomach as a feint. The ruse, properly executed, will fake an opponent into a vulnerable position. Once he takes the bait, then a crippling blow can be delivered to any target of opportunity.

The attack depicted in *Fig. 6* illustrates a cross slash used as a feint *(A)* which causes the opponent to give ground. In the process, he will generally raise his knife arm or hold it widespread to the side. When using the cross-slash feint, it is delivered full force (as it must be sufficiently believable to fool the opponent), but the knife arm is stopped just short of a normal arc. Instantaneously, the arm is then whipped up and backward, delivering a back slash to the throat (preferably) or any part

Figure 6(B).

of the face as a secondary target *(B)*. Whether the opponent has maintained his position (after evading the cross-slash feint) or moves to counterattack, the back slash to the throat/face will usually catch him off guard. But only if it is delivered in the split fraction of a second that his mind is focused on the feint to his stomach. Naturally, some men have faster reactions than others; it is entirely possible that an opponent could evade both the cross-slash feint and the back slash. In that event, the attacker should return to the Combat Stance and probe for a new opening.

The flow and movement of a knife fight unfolds with blinding speed. Yet the attacker must remain constantly aware of his opponent's body position, and in particular, the position of his knife arm. To a great extent, the position of an opponent's knife arm determines the tactics to be used by the attacker. If the opponent's knife arm extends forward at shoulder level (even though he had retreated from a cross slash) then he could easily flick the knife across at face level, which precludes the attacker mounting a sustained attack. On the other hand, if the knife arm is held back or out (which are common mistakes when evading a cross slash) then the opportunities for a sustained attack are virtually unlimited.

The attack illustrated in *Fig. 7* depicts a very effective method in which the *cross-slash feint* can be employed to cripple the opponent's knife arm. Upon delivering a feint to the stomach, the attacker instantly realizes that the opponent has raised his knife arm to a *partially* extended position *(A)*. Without hesitation, even while his arm is projected in the cross-slash arc, the attacker must immediately slash upward with great force. The blow can be directed to either the wrist or forearm, or the bicep muscles of the opponent's knife arm *(B)*. If delivered with sufficient force to sever tendons and/or arteries, this upward slash will automatically disarm the opponent and place the attacker in virtual control of the fight. It is entirely possible, of course, to execute the same upward cut if the opponent's arm is *fully* extended at shoulder level. Quite obviously, however, such a blow must be struck with remarkable speed. In the fractionalized moment that the attacker strikes upward to the knife arm, the opponent might very well deliver a cut to the face or throat.

NOTE: In most knife fights, the opponent's *left arm* is virtually ignored as a target. All too often, in the heat of the fight, the attacker simply forgets that the left arm is a vital body area. The radial and brachial arteries, along with assorted tendons on the forearm and hand, are no less life-supporting than those on the knife arm. Moreover, the opponent usually extends his left arm farther, and seldom guards it with equal caution. So the left arm is frequently vulnerable, and far more exposed than the knife arm. It is particularly susceptible to attack by delivering a cross-slash feint and then executing a back slash to the left forearm/wrist area. Another excellent tactic is a quick thrust-feint to the face followed by a downward cut to the left forearm/wrist/hand. An attack to the left arm is worth serious consideration, and should be added to your bag of tricks. It can end the fight almost as rapidly as a decisive blow to the knife arm.

It now becomes apparent, from the feint-and-slash tactics depicted in ***Figs.*** *5–7,* that a sustained attack can be mounted using little more than the basic cross slash and back slash. But if we grant the opponent equal skills, then some added refinement may be needed in an individual's knife fighting repertoire. As previously mentioned, your opponent will instinctively assume a defensive posture concerning his stomach. All the more so after you have slashed or feinted near his bellybutton. Thus, with his attention misdirected, he immediately becomes vulnerable to slashes aimed at the face/throat. Moreover, since he now expects a concerted attack to the midriff, he becomes mentally flustered when the blade is suddenly flicked in his face. This unanticipated danger is often more disconcerting than a minor wound; when a man abruptly finds a knife flashing near his throat, he usually adopts a whole new defensive attitude. That's the time to capitalize on the factor of surprise.

The attacker has already directed a series of blows to the stomach. Now he suddenly launches a cross slash to the face/throat. The opponent is caught off guard, and this unexpected attack might very well inflict a vital wound. Even if the opponent's reactions are quick enough to avoid the blow, it creates lingering intimidation, and he will quickly assume a defensive stance.

Figure 7(A).

Figure 7(B).

Once having used this tactic, the attacker can then add a subtle refinement (depicted in *Fig. 8*) by feinting a cross slash to the face *(A)*. As the blade passes the opponent's head, the attacker instantly slashes downward to the chest/stomach *(B)* or any target of opportunity. Though a slash wound on the upper chest seldom disables an opponent, it will rather quickly discourage him from becoming overly aggressive. The same downward slash might be directed instead to the arm or the armpit, which would bring the fight to a hasty conclusion.

When dealing with a particularly aggressive opponent, he will often slide away from your cross slash to the face/throat and immediately move forward to counterattack.

Figure 8(A).

In this event, the attacker should forego the downward slash, and instead back slash to the face/throat of his overeager opponent. While the various slashes aimed at the face/throat might miss the mark, the opponent will usually withdraw into a defensive stance. The attacker then dominates the situation, and can force the fight in a manner to his own advantage.

Obviously, the ability to mount a sustained attack requires that the attacker maintain the offensive and retain control of the fight. Of equal importance, he must have the mental awareness to ***instinctively*** deliver the correct blows in successive order. The defensive movements of an opponent, in particular his body position at any given

Figure 8(B).

moment, determine the next blow to be struck. The attacker must evaluate those movements on the instant, and then, without hesitation, slash or cut before the situation can change. The action in a particular knife fight will, of course, differ in specific sequence from that of any other encounter. However, the basic slash/feint/cut remains the same; the decisive factor is to put them together in a combination which capitalizes on the unfolding situation.

The sustained attack illustrated in *Fig. 9* is but one of countless possible combinations that might be used in any given knife fight. The series of blows struck by the attacker in this sequence, however, graphically depict a pattern of rapid, aggressive slashes. By forcing the action, the attacker can effectively keep his opponent off balance, retain the initiative and ultimately deliver the blow that ends the fight.

The attacker opens with a cross slash to the stomach *(A)* which his opponent has anticipated and easily evades. Sensing a counterattack, the attacker then back slashes to the stomach *(B)*, which has the immediate effect of halting the opponent's forward surge. Before his adversary can recover, the attacker strikes with an upward cross slash to the face/throat *(C)*. When his opponent slides away from the blow, he immediately follows with a downward back slash to the arms/chest/stomach *(D)*, which forces the man to give further ground. In complete control of the situation at this point, the attacker once more cross slashes to the stomach, which his harried adversary evades with somewhat less agility *(E)*. Then, as the opponent attempts to gain the initiative and counterattack, the attacker ends the fight with a quick, upward back slash to the throat *(F)*.

If properly executed, a sustained attack of this nature would require ten seconds or less to conclude. On the other hand, if the two men were evenly matched, then the

Figure 9(A).

Figure 9(B).

Figure 9(C).

advantage could shift back and forth between attack and counterattack until one of them blundered. Of vital importance is the fact that once the attacker delivered the opening blow, he aggressively forced the issue. There was never a moment's hesitation, nor did he allow the opponent to regain his balance. Instead, he constantly forced his adversary backwards by taking a short step forward (or circling) with each blow struck.

When assaulted by a determined and tenacious attacker, it is extremely difficult, regardless of a man's skill and/or reflexes, to gain control of the situation. All the more so once he has been forced into a defensive pattern. That thought alone leads to another cardinal rule: *An aggressive attack provides the ultimate defense in a knife fight.* Clearly, when a man is confronted with an antagonist brandishing a knife, survival dictates that he strike first and strike fast. Then he must aggressively press the fight with a series of chain-lightning slashes/cuts/thrusts that will force his opponent off balance and ultimately create an opening for the final blow.

Of course, as a practical matter, the reality of combat is hardly so cut and dried. There are very few men of such skill and determination that they will never find themselves on the defensive in a knife fight. The thought becomes a truth of no small consequence to the citizen who is attacked by a mugger or a robber on a dark street. The thug invariably has his knife out and ready for action when he accosts an unsuspecting victim. The individual faced with this situation has the choice of acceding to the hoodlum's demands, whatever they may be, or of fighting. The latter choice may very well offer the better odds for survival. Certainly, the criminal confronted by a resolute victim, who suddenly pulls a knife and escalates the situation to a fight on equal terms, will be momentarily disconcerted, to say the least. That initial moment of surprise might easily enable the victim to turn the tables,

Figure 9(D).

Figure 9(E).

Figure 9(F).

thereby seizing the aggressive role. The greater likelihood, however, is that the peaceful citizen, even after choosing to fight, will still find himself on the defensive. In that predicament, a knowledge of counterattack tactics becomes essential.

Counterattack is basically a matter of retreating, and avoiding an assailant's blade, until his attack has lost its momentum. Or else waiting until he blunders and inadvertently creates an opening for a counterblow. It requires agility, a clear head and the nerve to step in at the right moment. (Even though that forward movement will place you within the assailant's strike zone.) We have discussed ways that an individual can lure his assailant into a particular attack as a means of setting up a specific counterattack. These tactics demand skill and cunning, however, and they are not for the faint of heart. Until you're a blooded fighter, you should concentrate on the *basic* defensive moves that will draw an adversary forward. In a sense, you fool him, allow him to become confident that he is in complete control of the fight. By retreating, you play for time until the exact instant arrives for an aggressive counterstroke.

The successful counterattacker is nothing quite so much as a good actor. He retreats quickly, but only far enough to lure his assailant into continued attack. His defensive moves are exaggerated, conveying the impression that he overreacts and lacks coordination. He openly displays fear and an overpowering reluctance to engage in close-quarters combat. Finally, his limited attempts to retaliate are hesitant, ineffectual and half-hearted. All of which provokes contempt and false confidence within the assailant. For the individual who has never been subjected to a knife fight, most of these responses will come quite naturally. In fact, acting may never become necessary; the situation itself could easily prompt a genuine display of these same emotions. Nonetheless, the essen-

Figure 10(A).

tial requirement is to retreat quickly, but only far enough to evade the knife. In short, give ground but maintain the balance and mobility necessary to strike within the split-second that an opening presents itself.

The illustrations in *Fig. 10* depict an assailant attacking with a cross slash to the stomach. The individual retreating has jumped backward (allowing the blade to pass within inches of his abdomen) while simultaneously extending his knife arm at shoulder level *(A)*. Now is the precise instant for counterattack! While the assailant's knife arm is extended in a cross slash, he is momentarily vulnerable. However, the opening will exist for only a split fraction of a second. If the defender is to strike, it must be done *simultaneously* as the blade passes his

Figure 10(B).

stomach. To counterattack, the defender holds his position, without stepping further into the assailant's strike zone. Then he leans forward, extending his arm fully, and executes a cut to the face/throat *(B)*. All of this must be accomplished, however, in the instant prior to the assailant's delivering another blow. So if the defender's counterattack fails, he must then immediately withdraw to the Combat Stance. His arm/throat/stomach are exposed to attack; the assailant could easily step forward and execute a back slash. Should the counterattack succeed, of course, the defender will have gained the initiative and can quickly launch a sustained attack. A variation on this tactic is to wait until the assailant executes the back slash and then counterattack to the face/throat.

If anything, the counterattack illustrated in *Fig. 11* requires an even finer sense of timing. Not to mention a high degree of daring. The assailant has delivered a cross slash (either to the stomach or the face), and the defender has retreated only far enough to evade the blow *(A)*. Without hesitation, the defender moves forward and to the left at the exact instant the blade passes his body. Simultaneously, he grabs the assailant's elbow or arm and shoves it forcefully to the right. Then he steps in and delivers a full thrust to the stomach *(B)*. The last step is both tricky and imperative: the defender must immediately disengage, then slide away to the left and assume the Combat Stance. In this manner, he avoids all retaliation and leaves his assailant vitally wounded. The same maneuver is in order if he fails to gain control of the assailant's knife arm, since he is clearly vulnerable to a back slash. On the other hand, if the counterthrust is accomplished without mishap, then for all practical purposes the fight is finished.

The counterattack depicted in *Fig. 12* is a subtle refinement on those previously illustrated. It requires the nervy calculation to await and evade both a cross slash and a back slash. The assailant delivers a cross slash (either to the stomach or the face), and the defender retreats just beyond the strike zone *(A)*. No counteraction is taken at this time, so in a sense, the defender invites another blow. The assailant, as expected, executes a back slash. The defender avoids the blade by inches and simultaneously grabs the assailant's knife arm as it passes his body. Then he wrenches it to the left and steps forward, directing a full thrust to the stomach *(B)*. Again, the last step is vital. The defender immediately disengages; withdraws to the right; and assumes the Combat Stance. Of course, if the defender fails to obtain a firm grip on the assailant's knife arm, then he must withdraw in the same manner and await another opening.

Figure 11(A).

Figure 11(B).

Figure 12(A).

Figure 12(B).

NOTE: The counterattacks illustrated in *Figs. 10–12* are equally effective against a thrust attack. A full thrust (as opposed to a flicking thrust) requires that substantial body weight be committed on the right foot. So in actual combat, with the assailant slightly off balance and his knife arm extended, it is often simpler to grab his arm in the thrust position than in the slash position. Also, bear in mind, the counterattacks depicted in *Figs. 10–12* can be directed to *any* target of opportunity. Instead of countering with a thrust, the defender could easily deliver a cut to the arm/wrist or face/throat. The idea is to strike and strike fast—anywhere—but make it a blow that counts!

A word of caution. When a defender grabs the knife arm of an assailant *(Figs. 11 & 12)*, it is entirely possible that his own knife arm will be grasped. The risk becomes all the greater unless the defender's counterthrust follows *simultaneously* upon having grabbed his assailant's knife arm. The timing on these moves leaves little room for error; if the counterattack is to succeed, then the thrust must coincide exactly with clutching the assailant's arm and shoving it aside. So beware and be prepared. It could get very sticky.

In the event the assailant *does* grab the defender's knife arm *(Fig. 13)*, then the defender must immediately drift backwards. The gambit here is to retreat as though being forced to give ground, luring the assailant into a movement which builds forward body momentum. After retreating two or three steps, the defender falls backward, pulling his assailant forward by the arm. Then he plants his feet in the assailant's stomach and lifts him overhead with a piston-like kick of the legs *(A)*. If executed properly, this overhead lift will drop the assailant three or four feet away with stunning impact. When the defender kicks upward, he should release the assailant's knife arm and scramble to his feet the moment the overhead lift is

Figure 13(A).

Figure 13(B).

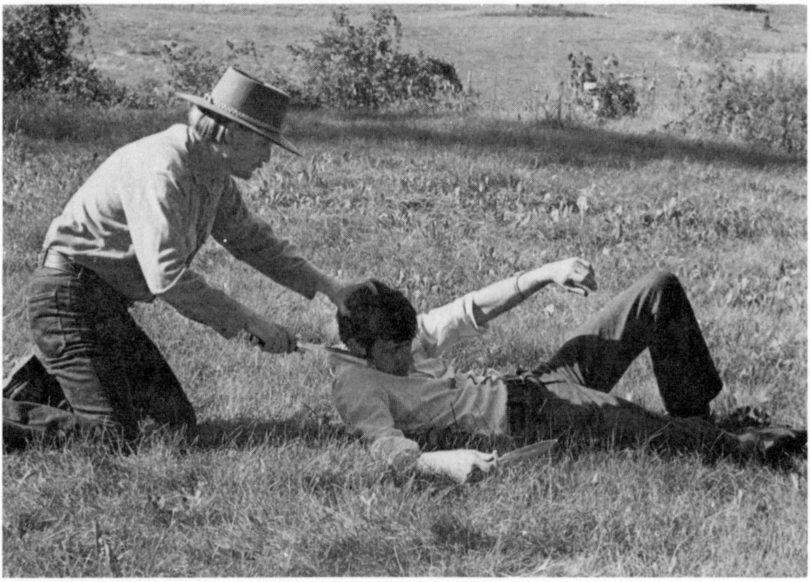

completed. Timed correctly, the defender can roll and be on his feet within a second of the assailant's hitting the ground. Swiftly, he then closes the gap and directs a slash and/or thrust to any target of opportunity *(B)*.

The instinctive reaction, when two men grab one another's knife arm, is to wrestle and shove in an attempt to wrench free. Thus, when the defender initially gives ground, it will be interpreted as a sign of weakening. In order to capitalize on the ruse, the defender must retreat immediately and execute the overhead lift before his assailant becomes suspicious. This maneuver is far less risky than it appears at first glance. The real hazard is that an assailant of greater physical strength might very well wrench his knife arm free if the struggle continued—while he still has hold of ***your*** knife arm! So don't hesitate. Executed swiftly, the overhead lift rarely fails, and with survival at stake, it's well worth the risk.

The occasion may arise, of course, in which a citizen is attacked without warning. Or attacked so aggressively, perhaps, that he has no chance for an immediate counter blow. In this situation, the defender must retreat steadily, but without panic, and await the moment an opening presents itself. The sequence depicted in *Fig. 14* illustrates a sustained attack in which the defender retreats a step at a time. Slowly giving ground, he avoids in succession a cross slash to the face/throat *(A);* then a downward slash to the chest *(B);* followed by a cross slash to the stomach *(C),* and finally, a back slash to the throat. At that point, the assailant's momentum has faltered. The defender has quickly moved forward (as the knife passed his face in the back slash) and grabbed the assailant's arm. Then he has shoved it firmly to the left and simultaneously stepped in with a full thrust to the stomach *(D)*. These illustrations are meant to convey some understanding of the movements and tactics employed in counterattack. But in no way should it be inferred that all such encoun-

Figure 14(A).

Figure 14(B).

ters end as swiftly and cleanly as depicted. Quite the contrary, in fact, for those involved.

History records numerous knife fights which lasted a quarter hour or longer. Generally, before one of the adversaries had made a fatal mistake, both men had been cut repeatedly. Engagements with a knife are often prolonged affairs simply because the participants understand the rudiments of the game; both are wary of making a fatal blunder, and they each have the necessary skills to withstand a sustained attack. The counterattacks depicted, however, demonstrate that a resolute defender, who retreats without becoming flustered and strikes decisively at the opportune moment, has an excellent chance to thwart the attack of a determined assailant. Of course, there are no guarantees.

A defender might find himself attacked so relentlessly that he hasn't the opportunity to mount even the slightest counterattack. Discretion being the better part of valor, he must then retreat fast enough and far enough so that the assailant has no choice but to approach and open the engagement anew. Although back-pedaling in this fashion does little for the ego, it provides a man with a fresh start and another chance to assume the aggressor's role. On occasion, when it's a matter of run or get cut, it may be the only stratagem left to a hard-pressed defender.

THE DO AND DON'T CHECKLIST. A skilled knife fighter would be the first to admit that mastering the blade is a never-ending process. There are no absolutes—anything goes! To survive, a man must constantly expand his knowledge of attack and counterattack. So perhaps a few random observations—tips of the trade—would prove beneficial at this point. Since no man tells all, you might correctly surmise that certain things can be learned *only* in personal combat.

Figure 14(C).

Figure 14(D).

Do search out and study the written works of other knife fighters. You might very well discover a technique or some sage piece of advice that could one day save your life.

Do encourage your wife to learn the self-defense techniques of knife fighting. Women often have faster reaction time than men, and they possess all the strength necessary to deliver an effective slash/cut/thrust. Moreover, women can be tough as nails, particularly in defense of the home. When the chips are down, they usually approach a threatening situation with a cunning, no-nonsense attitude about tactics. So they make dangerous adversaries! A single woman, living alone, has all the more reason to master the knife. It might very well be the only weapon available, and her life, if not her honor, certainly justifies the risk of a knife fight.

Do practice the techniques of knife fighting on a regular basis. It requires only a few minutes a day, and the practice sessions can be held in your own living room. Trim several sheets of newspaper to the length of your knife; roll the sheets into a tight tube, and bind the tube with rubber bands. Now you have an instrument roughly the size and weight of your knife, but its slash/cut/thrust effect is relatively harmless. Practice every evening with your wife as an opponent, and you can both learn together. Then you'll be a formidable family indeed! But however you accomplish it, practice until you have mastered the basics of attack and counterattack. Otherwise, the first time you pull a knife on an armed assailant might very well be the last.

Do avoid further engagement once you have seriously wounded an assailant. Circle and feint. Keep him scared and on the defensive. Force him to move and pump blood and keep on moving until he drops. It might take a minute or so but then he's down and out, finished off by sheer loss of blood. So take your time and let nature take its course. Avoid being wounded—or killed—by a man whose ticker is about to stop.

Don't underestimate your assailant's skill with a knife. Enter the engagement with the very firm conviction that he's a holy terror, the damnedest knife fighter since James Bowie went under at the Alamo. Never fear being cut, but at the same time, never assume you will be cut. Assume instead that he's dangerous and knows all the tricks of attack and counterattack. If he doesn't, then you're home free. If he does, then remember that pearl of wisdom previously mentioned. Be swift and be careful!

Don't enter your assailant's strike zone unless you are on the attack. Perhaps it will be nothing more than a slash/feint/slash or a quick thrust to a target of opportunity. Or perhaps it will be the opening blow in a sustained attack. But you must *never* enter his strike zone unless you control the action. If your attack loses momentum, then withdraw immediately to the Combat Stance. Conversely, never allow the assailant to enter *your* strike zone with impunity. Perhaps you will be forced to retreat. If he's skilled and aggressive, you might be hard-pressed to stave off a sustained attack. But when his attack falters—by virtue of your elusiveness and mobility—never allow him to *leave* your strike zone unassailed. Counterattack anything within reach. A quick cut to the face. A slash to the arm or hand. A short, jabbing thrust to the chest or stomach. Hit something—anything—but punish him before he leaves your strike zone. However slight the wound you inflict, let him know that he can't get away in one piece. Next time, he'll be a lot more careful when he attacks. So punish him, draw blood, make him wary of your blade. Then you've got the battle half won.

Don't toss your knife from hand to hand in imitation of street gang punks. It rarely fools anyone, or flusters them, and a knife blow delivered with the left hand is usually so ineffective as to be worthless. Of greater consequence, when passing the knife from hand to hand, you are momentarily *unarmed!* A skilled knife fighter would cut your throat while the knife is in mid-air. Then he would wonder where you had learned such an asinine stunt, and he'd be right.

Don't throw your knife in imitation of movie tough guys. It looks great on film, but in real life it simply doesn't work. In a combat situation, the ability to stick a knife point first, not to mention throwing it with any degree of accuracy, is so negligible as to constitute suicide. If you throw your knife, you have only *one* chance. That's it! No retakes. And if you miss, then you'd better be prepared to outrun an adversary who has wisely retained his own blade. But if you simply can't resist the temptation, then don't practice knife throwing, practice sprinting.

Knife fighting is a cruel, vicious business. Anyone who manages to extricate himself, even if it means outrunning his assailant, will have avoided one of the most unpleasant experiences known to man. With remarkable frequency, even the winner of a knife fight resembles a freshly butchered side of beef; police files are studded with reports of engagements in which both participants ended up on a morgue slab. The only favorable commentary that might be made is the fact that an individual, confronted by a knife-wielding assailant, has few options. The blade in his own hand may well represent his *one* chance for survival.

The homeowner or citizen walking the streets after dark would doubtless go to extreme lengths to avoid a knife fight. However, in today's society it is not at all uncommon for a man to be subjected to the ordeal. So if your number comes up, remember the first tenet of all veteran knife fighters. *A sustained, aggressive attack provides both the best defense and the greatest likelihood of living to a ripe old age.*

The five inflexible rules for survival in a knife fight:

1. Strike first and strike fast whenever threatened by a knife-wielding assailant.

2. Carry the fight to your assailant; maintain the initiative, and deny him the chance to mount an attack.

3. When attacking, advance only one step at a time. Never lunge! Circle your assailant and be evasive; force him to fight *your* fight.

4. Consider an assailant dangerous so long as he is standing or capable of offering resistance of any nature.

5. When forced on the defensive, time your retreat to the pace of the attack, and remain constantly on the alert for *any* opening that will allow you to counterattack.

APPENDIX

Weapons Summary

1. PISTOLS

Automatics

Perhaps the most widely known automatics are those manufactured by Browning, Colt and Smith & Wesson. All are available in either .38 Super or 9mm and hold up to 14 shots. However, there are several fine gun manufacturers who market comparable products. One of the newest, and certainly one of the finest, is the Star PD .45 Auto marketed by the Garcia Corporation. Similarly, there are a number of excellent, small-framed automatics manufactured in .380 caliber. Check with your local gun dealer for a full listing and current availability.

Revolvers

Old names dominate, and here again, Colt and Smith & Wesson are widely respected. However, several firms offer quality revolvers, nearly all manufactured in either .38 Special or .357 Magnum with 4″ barrel. Visit your local gun dealer for a full listing and current availability.

2. SHOTGUNS

Pump

The Ithaca Model 37 Deerslayer and the Remington Model 870 Bushmaster are perhaps the most widely known 20″ barrel pump (slide action) shotguns. Yet several fine manufacturers offer pump scatterguns, and any reputable gunsmith can adjust the barrel length to your satisfaction.

Double Barrel

Nearly all American double barrel shotguns have standard long tubes, including the Savage/Fox Model B and the Savage/Stevens Model 311. However, any reliable gunsmith can shorten the barrels within the limits of the law. Also, scatterguns such as the Rossi Overland and the Universal TOZ-66 come with 20″ barrels and exposed hammers.

3. KNIVES

Sheath Knives

W.D. (Bo) Randall is unquestionably the most famous custom knifemaker in the world. However, there are upwards of 200 custom knifemakers in the United States, and the majority are capable of fashioning a fighting knife to your specifications. For an inexpensive, over-the-counter product, you could hardly do better than a replica Fairbairn-Sykes Commando Knife. Check with your local gun dealer or sporting goods store for a complete list of custom knifemakers.

Folding Hunter or Jackknife

Any gun shop or sporting goods store carries a line of manufactured folding knives. Some of the more popular brands are Browning, Buck, Rigid and Gerber. Also, you can order a custom-made folding hunter from any one of dozens of knifemakers. Price and quality are the determining factors, so visit a few stores and talk knives before making a decision.

4. WATCHDOGS

Beware of self-professed dog trainers. Call the K-9 Unit of your local police department or the sheriff's department. Ask for advice and the name of the nearest trainer who is a member of the Professional Dog Trainers Association. There are no bargain watchdogs; a reliable dog is a professionally trained dog, and that represents a major investment. So seek advice and take your time. If you have difficulty in locating a reliable trainer, write me c/o The Devin-Adair Publishing Co., Old Greenwich, Conn. 06870, and I will provide the necessary information.

ABOUT THE AUTHOR

Matt Braun was born in Oklahoma, and spent a good part of his boyhood on a ranch. Along the way, he lived in Oklahoma, Texas, Arizona, New Mexico, Kansas and Colorado. During his youth and early manhood, he was constantly involved with members of the Osage and Cherokee tribes. Commenting on the relationship, Braun states: "We ate and slept together, sometimes fought one another, and spent every spare moment off in the woods hunting. I developed an abiding respect for Indians during this period. They made magnificent friends and formidable enemies; their philosophy regarding the right of each man to walk his own path became my own. A quarter century has passed, but I still look back on that time as one of the highwater marks of my life."

Coincidentally, a branch of his family, the Adairs, played a distinguished role in the history of the Cherokee nation. The founder of the Cherokee Adairs, James Adair, wrote the definitive work on the Five Civilized Tribes.

The book, entitled *The History of the American Indians*, was published in London in 1775, and a year later James Adair married into the Cherokee tribe.

Altogether Braun served four years as a noncom and an officer in the U.S. Army. After Ranger training, he taught survival techniques to the troops (including firearms, knife fighting and hand-to-hand combat), and received a letter of commendation from the Commanding General for his proficiency as an instructor.

After graduating from college with a degree in journalism, and serving a hitch in the army, Braun worked briefly on a newspaper. Then he entered the business world, and spent several years in corporate journalism. Finally, in 1969, he decided it was time to start doing what he'd always wanted to do: write historical novels about the West. He resigned from the business world and spent two years holed up in the mountains learning how—and how not—to write novels. The first three efforts remain unpublished; his break came in early 1972 when two novels were bought by separate publishers within a matter of two weeks. Since then, eleven novels and one nonfiction work have been published.

Although active in several professional organizations, Braun continues to live in a remote section of mountains. He hunts at every opportunity—both with rifle and bow and arrow—and stays in shape with jogging, riding horses, and backpack camping trips. Currently forty-four years old, his weight is exactly the same (160 lbs.) as when he fought in the middleweight division of the Golden Gloves. Also, he works out regularly on a combat pistol course, and can consistently draw/fire/score on a silhouette target in 4/10 of a second. On occasion, he devotes time to survival training courses for civilians, which includes instruction on home security and personal self-defense.

Braun's wife, Bettiane, began her career as a ballet

dancer, later appeared in several Broadway musicals, and was featured in a number of television shows. After that she became a successful model, and upon leaving New York began a new career as a consultant with a French cosmetics company. An eager pupil of self-defense, she is now qualified to defend herself with firearms, knives, and hand-to-hand combat techniques.

The Save-Your-Life Defense Handbook stands as testament to Braun's belief that "crime prevention starts at home," and evolved from his personal conviction that every man has a moral obligation to defend family and home.